Wheel ... ce

My Li... Cerebral Palsy

Suzie Dru Drury

Rosie Dru Drury

For you, Pips.

We have shared so much, so I write my story for you.

Contents

About the Author

Suzie lives in Wiltshire where she enjoys an independent life within a small town outside of Salisbury, with family and friends living close by. Following a passion for poetry, Suz decided to put more words to paper and began to write about her life, living with cerebral palsy.

Suz has a wicked sense of humour and has created some awesome sayings that are unique to her, all included in this book, along with her novel poetry that she has been writing over the years.

Suz has worked with her sister, Rosie, to write this book, so that she can share with the reader, a life living with cerebral palsy and all that comes with having a disability; experiences that an able-bodied person might not always understand, but which are interesting and thought provoking.

DruZooBooks

First published October 2022
www.druzoobooks.com
First published in Great Britain by DruZooBooks
Printed by Kindle Direct Publishing
Edited by Book Helpline

A catalogues record for this book is available from the British Library.

ISBN 978-0-9927579-4-6

Acknowledgments

My parents, for always supporting me, giving advice and helping me to reflect my experiences and memories in a written format. Also, for helping with the initial editing and correcting any false memories!

My sister, Rosie, for being my ghost writer and encouraging me to write about my life.

My brother-in-law, Barry, for designing the front and back cover of this book, and for taking such a beautiful photo of a sunset across Salisbury City, capturing Salisbury Cathedral.

My sister, Jenny, for always been there during some hard times, and visiting me in hospital on a number of occasions where I have had to stay in overnight.

To Bry, for always supporting me, and for taking a photo of me, by a rock, to symbolise the obstacles that I have overcome in my life.

Wheels of Independence

A bright idea came to my mind one day
"WATCH OUT" a book is on the way
My mind is buzzing I have to say
I will start without delay.

I load "Wordpad" on my PC
Writing on this, is easier for me
My monitor is big you see
So I'm able to read the print easily
And alter the paragraphs frequently.

I've never done a book before
Off to the internet I go to explore
What came up didn't interest me at all
So it was time to withdraw.

I'll give Rose a call, she'll be a good mentor
I need further assistance after all
I've hit a brick wall, and I'm about to fall
One day I will be on the ball.

Within a minute my confidence came back
"WOW", it's a YES, I am now on the right track
I can achieve the goal I've been looking at
I'm so thankful for that, and the good chat.

I take myself down memory lane
Instantly I remember pain
Which was a tremendous strain
I'm a positive person in the main
And I have so much more to gain.

Then the title of my book came
Oh I'm on my good luck chain
I'm hoping this is where I will remain
"Wheels of Independence" well done brain
It's moving faster than a train.

Having a disability is hard to explain
It's like constantly losing a game
The frustration is always the same
This is a shame but, no ones to blame
"Determined Suz" is a nickname.

I have managed to ski
And I live independently
Challenges are good for me
It keeps my mind active you see
Which helps me move forward happily.

Writing has helped me so much actually
How I feel comes out automatically
And all my worries disappear rapidly
I've finished "Wheels of Independence" finally.

Chapter 1

Introduction

Imagine if we were able to choose our life. What culture would we choose? What skin colour, hair colour, ethnicity would we choose? What would we want our personality to be like? What would we want out of life? What friends would we like to have? Where would we like to live and in what part of the world?

Endless questions which we can indulge ourselves in, but we do not always have these choices or the option to change what our life is to be. We are born who we are and dealt our life cards, and whatever is on these cards, we must make the most of it. Our childhood experiences shape who we are, and we have little control over them. Our caregivers, whether they be our parents, our extended family, grandparents, aunts, uncles or the teachers who influence us at school, will be the ones who begin to shape personality and consequently, the tapestry of our life.

Cerebral palsy, however, was not influenced by anyone or a result of any childhood experience. It was simply part of my life. These were my life cards that I had to play.

Living a life with cerebral palsy has been challenging, but a challenge such as this cannot be faced lightly, and from somewhere I found the determination and strength to meet this challenge head-on. Whether it was the support and nurturing from my family that gave me the confidence I needed or just my upbringing – maybe my genealogy – I can't be sure, but I have approached my life with this attitude, with this determination, and it has served me well.

I write this at forty-seven years of age. I was born on the 8th of December 1972, in Germany, in a place called Rinteln Hospital. At the time, my father was in the army, posted to Germany and was living in Lemgo with my mother and my eldest sister, Jenny. Rinteln was the British military hospital in that part of Germany.

I am a twin, and I have one elder sister and one younger sister. My elder sister was only born eleven months before me and my twin, and my younger sister was born four years later. Growing up with three sisters meant that there was never a dull moment for any of us! I also do not think we can fully appreciate what it was like for my parents to have four children under the age of five, with three of those children being nearly the same age! It was a happy home and I have some very fond memories, which I will share in the following chapters.

Living with cerebral palsy does not define me, but it is part of me. By not defining me, I mean that I am still Suz, a person outside of a disability. I am still the Suz I probably would have been without cerebral palsy. People often ask how I would describe myself. My answer is, I enjoy having a laugh, I love being around people and I like to help people as much as I can. This means a lot to me. Over the years I have had help when I have needed it, and I just want to be able to repay that kindness and be there as a friend for anyone who might need the support.

I have never known a life without having to walk with sticks. When I was younger, you could say that my sticks were my second pair of legs; I could not go anywhere without them. When

I first started to walk, I had tripods, and then as I grew older, I was given sticks. In my later years, I spent more time in a wheelchair because cerebral palsy has this way of reducing your mobility as you get older, but I still try to do some walking every day. I also have an exercise bike, which is another good way to exercise, particularly because it focuses on the knees, and the process of folding my legs at the knees is beneficial. Trying to walk and exercise regularly keeps my joints and muscles supple and moving, which is important if I want to keep my circulation active.

It must be very difficult for people to understand what life is like being so restricted, not only in movement but also restricted in the ability to go somewhere, make plans; sometimes to have fun! Why would they understand; why would they have to understand? However, when faced with the challenges that I have, it makes me want other people to understand what I go through so that they can appreciate their independence, an independence that a person might feel robbed of when they have cerebral palsy.

This book will not reflect me feeling sorry for myself; it will tell my story and it will touch upon those areas of a life living with cerebral palsy that are somewhat different from what an able-bodied person might experience.

I also write about my school days and how I grew up around people with other disabilities, some more debilitating than mine, others less so, and some that were very similar because they also had cerebral palsy, but the cerebral palsy manifested itself in a different way. I write about my best friends, how close and connected we all were. They were like sisters to me. Two of my best friends had a life-limiting disability. Experiencing grief at such a young age when they both passed away in their teenage years was very difficult for me. However, I also recall the fun that we had at school. The way we lived our life as any other schoolgirl or schoolboy would, misbehaving in the same way, being cheeky, testing the boundaries in the same way, experimenting in the same way.

My twin sister, Pips, is a huge part of my life. Being a twin brings with it a profound sense of belonging. We shared so many months in a womb together, in a miracle closeness that although cannot be remembered, leaves a subconscious bond that is undeniable.

We had a busy childhood! We were very lucky to travel as a family; some brief holidays in the UK and Europe, and another more exotic location in Zimbabwe. Again, it was not always straightforward for me to travel and to live in different places, but I have many wonderful memories and experiences, which I recall later in this book.

Growing into adulthood with cerebral palsy again came with its challenges, which I embraced. I achieved full-time employment, which was so rewarding, but when these opportunities were reduced and eventually subsided completely, it left a feeling of loss and rejection. I write about the illness that overtook me following the loss of full-time work, a significant time in my life, which changed me. I got through it with the support of my family, and I discovered a newfound hobby and talent in writing poetry. I will include a poem at the end of each chapter of this book.

I worked hard to recover from the illness, only to find that heartache awaited me. I could not complete this book without writing about grief. No one asks to experience grief, nobody wants to experience grief, and often, grief is unexpected, as it was for me. Sadly, dying is a fact of life and therefore most of us will experience the loss of a loved one at one point or another. Grief is a profound human emotion; grief makes us human! If we did not feel, and we did not grieve, then we would not have loved; and to love is a blessing. As with all the challenges that life throws, I had to face my grief head-on and find a way through it.

I will leave the introduction there and begin my story, but not before including a poem that I wrote about myself and my want for independence and how I felt when that independence arrived.

Independent Suz

Living independently is what I have always wanted to do
In 1993 my dream came true
I was excited and nervous too
But I knew I could achieve it
Even with the hurdles I may go through
It's going to be so cool.

My flat is small but I can't have it all
I love seeing my poems on my achievement wall
It gives me "A BUZZ" for sure
So I will get on and write some more.

When I clean, I'm a music machine
I sing away, poor neighbours, that's all I can say
The Hoover lead always gets in my way
My legs don't want to play, so no skipping for today
"You've Been Framed" would laugh away
"Independent Suz" could be famous one day.

Chapter 2

Twins

I have a twin sister. Her name is Pippa, although most people called her Pips. We are fraternal twins, which means we are not identical and did not share a placenta. Therefore, our genetic composition is different, and we have different blood types. However, people have often said to both Pips and me that they can tell we are twins.

There is something very special about being a twin. There is an unspoken connection, an unexplained bond. For all those months to be in such a confined space, sensing the other's existence, responding to their movements, feeling their touch, hearing their presence. It is the experience of a closeness that cannot be described because it is a memory stored firmly and deeply within the subconscious mind, irretrievable when we get plunged into the life that is on earth. However, it is real, those feelings, that presence, it is there, it was there, and it stays with us. Just because there are no conscious memories does not make it any less profound.

It presents itself in our life all the time. Despite Pips and I being independent people, having our own life, our own friends, our own ambitions, and a different direction in life, we still always felt a closeness, although we still had our moments where we argued! It was important to us that we were independent and different, whilst at the same time feeling our connection, having those similarities that only twins can have.

I have cerebral palsy, so my life was always going to be different to Pips; Pips is abled-bodied. We did not go to the same school; my parents would have liked us to, but it was not possible because most schools at the time were just not well-equipped enough. I needed physiotherapy, for example, on a regular basis. The school that Pips went to did not have that facility.

I know that Pips found it hard to see me struggling with my disability on a day-to-day basis. It was that battle I had between wanting to be independent whilst needing practical help that she understood. She knew how important independence was to me.

'Why is it so important though?' a friend once said. 'Just let people help more!'

'It's important because I can't always rely on people being around me,' I would reply. 'And what if they're not around?' I would challenge.

To my own question, I would respond, 'Then I would have to do whatever it is, myself!'

Even if I am struggling, the most important thing is that I can get there in the end. It may take me half an hour longer to do whatever it is I am doing, but it is about achieving it; that is where I get the 'buzz'.

Pips was always there for me, as were my other sisters. At any social gathering, they would always make sure that I had a drink and a plate of food before they got any for themselves. They knew how frustrating it was for me to see everyone else tucking into the buffet before I could even get a chance to wheel myself over. They knew, without me needing to explain, how difficult it was to tackle the plates along with reaching across the table to pick out some food, and then soon after pouring myself a drink. They were always there, thinking ahead and making sure that I wasn't the last in the queue, that I wasn't finding it hard to manage what someone who was able-bodied could so easily do … like helping themselves to food at a buffet!

Even on the day that she got married, Pips kept an eye on me. A day I remember so well. She married Barry in St Dennis, a sweet little church in a quaint village on the Cornish/Devon border called North Tamerton. It was a typically stormy and wet autumnal day, in early October, but this didn't detract from a beautiful service and then later, a lively evening reception about twenty miles away from the church, in the stunning Lanteglos Hotel. The guests arrived at the Lanteglos Hotel to enjoy a champagne-and-canapés reception and the long-awaited speeches from the best man, my father, and Barry, the groom himself. After this, an evening full of food, drinks and dancing awaited us. When it was time to delve into the huge buffet of food, it was Pips who made sure I was one of the first guests to get a plate.

At the end of the evening when Pips and Barry were about to leave in their limousine, which was going to take them from Cornwall to Heathrow airport, she could not find me to say goodbye because I had gone to the bathroom. This would have been the last time she would have seen me before going on her honeymoon. I remember fondly how she insisted on waiting until she had seen me; she told me she would not go on her honeymoon until she had said goodbye to me.

A couple of years after Pips and Barry married, Pips gave birth to her beautiful daughter, Evangeline. I remember her calling me to tell me. I was so pleased for her and Barry. I knew how much it meant to Pips, how much she had always wanted her own family, her own children. She had spent many years as a nanny, looking after other people's children, but she had always wanted her own.

The time surrounding Evangeline's birth was not easy though. Pips had to go into hospital a few weeks before her due date because she had high blood pressure. This naturally made

Pips anxious and consequently increased her blood pressure further. She called me from the hospital, and I could hear in her voice how worried she was about some of the complications. The professionals were suggesting an induction as they were worried for both Pips' health and her baby's health. Eventually, the decision was made to induce the birthing process and Evangeline was born safely and healthy. Unfortunately, Pips, blood pressure issues continued after the pregnancy, which was frustrating and worrying for her, as all Pips wanted to do, was to go home with her husband and daughter to begin their family life. She had to remain in hospital for a while longer. We talked again on the phone, and I tried to reassure her that she and Evangeline would be fine and that at least for now they were in the right place. I could tell by the end of our phone conversation that she was calmer. She did eventually get home and her blood pressure stabilised.

Pips and I had an element of 'twin telepathy', which can be quite common with twins. We were always quite good at reading one another's mind. However, it did not stop at that! Although we went to different schools, we used to take any opportunity to call each other for a catch-up. On one occasion, I mentioned that I had booked a date for my driving test. I did not realise that Pips had also applied for her driving test. As fate would have it, we were booked to do our driving tests on the same day, albeit at different times and in a different place. We were both amazed at the chances of that happening, but we were pleased that it did. It was awesome! When Pips passed her test and I did not, it meant that I could still celebrate that day, because I was so proud of her for passing. I didn't give in and went on to take another test shortly after, which I passed. We both ended up with a Fiat car; mine was red and Pips was white.

Other, more subtle events happened at the same time. For example, when we were younger, the same tooth fell out on the same day! Once, we ended up in hospital at the same time for different issues. I was having an operation and Pips went into hospital because of tummy pains. Just little subtleties like that, which made us smile given that we were twins, and we were experiencing similar situations for different reasons, but at the same time!

I remember when Pips broke her arm, I really felt her pain. Having been through so many operations myself, I really understood what she was going through, and because she was my twin, it was as if I felt it at a deeper level. With emotional pain, when Pips was upset, or when life was not going well for her, I found that it upset me greatly too.

Pips surprised me once on our birthday. What she did for me was a real example of how well she knew me, and how she understood what this surprise would mean to me. I had always wanted to meet the radio presenter Chris Ewington, who produced a show on our local radio. He made me laugh so much in the mornings when I listened to him. Pips asked me to meet her in town on our birthday, which of course I wanted to do, as we always tried to see each other on our birthday. When I met with her, she said, 'I have a surprise. Come with me!'

We walked a little way across town, and we arrived at a building with the sign 'Spire FM' outside. I slowly realised where we were, and I could feel the excitement in me rising!

'Are we going in here?' I asked Pips.

'We certainly are!' she replied.

Chris was waiting for us! It was just wonderful to see him in person, having listened to his voice for so long on the radio. Pips knew Chris because he lived opposite her. I was so touched that she thought to arrange this for me. We all giggled our way up a flight of stairs, both Pips and Chris helping me along. I saw the whole studio and the radio presenters in action! It was just awesome, and it is a memory that I will never forget.

Pips really did know me well. Our twin connection at the

forefront once again. Pips is 'one in a million' and I wrote this for us.

Twins

Pips likes to run
She finds it so much fun
To jog to the beat
When she's on her feet
She doesn't miss a beat
It makes her feel calm
So she is ready for a glass of wine
Which is so good for one's mind.

Suz wheels along
But doesn't keep up for long
And thinks I must keep strong
She does wheelies here and there
But her brakes aren't being fair
So she can't stop
And thinks "Oh my gosh I'm going to hit a rock"
Or even the end of the block.

Pips wins the race
A big smile increases on her face
When we touch base
She congratulates me
And this means a lot to me.

Pips and Suz
Don't always have the same views
Which can lead to big fumes
But deep down in my heart
There is always a special part

For you, that will never be torn apart
Onwards and upwards we go
As Suz likes going with the flow.

I hope from now on
We will keep going strong
Which will go on and on and on
And we can sing ding dong ding dong.

When times are hard
We mustn't put up a guard
But talk to each other
Because we do have love
That is spread from above
Just like two sparkling stars
That can be seen as far away as Mars.

This poem is coming to the end
And I hope it hasn't sent you around the bend
But I want to put things on the mend
So I send this and lots of love
And hope it will carry us through
This poem is written especially for you.

Chapter 3

Cerebral palsy

When I was born, I had a lack of oxygen and stopped breathing for about a minute. This could have resulted in me having cerebral palsy, although it was never determined that this was, in fact, the cause; there are other problems, which can occur in the brain during foetal development, or during birth, which could result in the same outcome. So, the cause of cerebral palsy will never be fully understood, but what was always certain was that I had it, and it wasn't going to go away.

The type of cerebral palsy I have is spastic cerebral palsy. This mainly affects my legs and my coordination. In very simple terms, it means that the messages from my brain that tell my legs to move do not get to my legs quick enough. I was also born with a squint in my left eye. It was my mother who first noticed it. She realised that I reacted to her voice, but it didn't look as if I could see her. I was eleven months old when I had a significant operation that successfully corrected this. But it didn't come without risk, and I was lucky to have the operation when I was so young, as it wasn't usual to do this operation on an eleven-month-old. One of my doctors at the time really encouraged it, telling my parents that it would help me, and it did. My parents tell me that

I was a different, much happier baby after this. I could now clearly see my family; most importantly, I could see my 'complete' mother.

However, it was not possible to correct cerebral palsy as easily, although I did have a couple of operations to help with my mobility, which I will recount later in this chapter. When you look at me, you'll see that I can walk, but only with two sticks.

A recollection I have that I think makes me smile, although it also makes me wonder what other people actually think cerebral palsy is, was when I was walking past someone, and they stopped me and said, 'What's wrong with you?'

I said, 'I have cerebral palsy, which is a lack of oxygen at birth.'

They replied, 'So, have you still got oxygen?'

Oh dear, I really was not sure what else to say! If I had not have laughed, I might well have cried!

The story of our birth is an interesting one. At the end of 1972, my father was fighting the Irish Republican Army in Northern Island and my mother was pregnant with Pips and me and was living in Germany at the time. My eldest sister, Jenny, was eleven months old. As my father had been away for over six months, he had only spent the first five months of Jen's life with her. This was army life!

The shock came when my father returned home on December 7th, met by my mother at the airport, who then promptly went into labour that night, at about 2.30am. The labour had started two months too early, although at the time, my parents weren't aware that this was dangerously early. In those days, there wasn't the knowledge that we have today; there wasn't such a constant check on the dates and how many weeks a woman had been pregnant.

The labour, by all accounts, was progressing quickly, so my father, with some urgency, made his way over to the army medical centre. There weren't any telephones and no mobile phones in the quarters that my parents were living in. How times have changed!

The medical team rapidly prepared the ambulance and drove my mother, under the blue flashing lights, to Rinteln British military hospital. Jenny and my father stayed at home, to manage as best as they could. My father hadn't been in the country for six months and had never set foot into their new home, so he had some familiarisation to do; both with looking after an eleven-month-old baby and with finding his way around the special abode that my mother had excitedly been preparing for him. However, he wasn't alone in this situation; as is typical of army life, there was a huge support network for my parents from the army, with endless wives arriving at the front door asking if they could help to look after Jenny. For my father, there was no panic. As far as he was concerned, his wife was making her way to the hospital to birth their second child.

My parents didn't know that my mother was carrying twins. In those days there was not the equipment; baby heart monitors, for example, or sonographs to discover how many little beings a mother is nurturing, yet alone to tell parents what gender their baby is. Today, women can ask for regular scanning, just for reassurance that the pregnancy is progressing well. If it were known that my mother was carrying twins, it wouldn't have been suggested that she give birth in a military hospital. Instead, she would have travelled back to England or have gone to a German hospital.

The journey to the military hospital took forty-five minutes and the birth started in the ambulance. My parents recall that the ambulance got brought to a halt at a level crossing. This must have been a fairly tense few minutes, particularly as it was just my mother and the male army medical orderly in the back of the ambulance, who had never delivered a baby. Once at the hospital, they rushed my mother inside, just in time for Pippa to be born. Pippa was born at a tiny weight of 2lbs and 12 ounce, and the nurses took her immediately to a special care unit. My mother was asked to give her newborn baby a name and was told to expect the worst.

Following the birth of Pippa, a nurse noticed that my mother's womb was still contracting and so continued to do some checks. A look of concern crossed her face whilst listening through the stethoscope that was placed on my mother's tummy.

'I can hear another heartbeat,' she said.

The doctors and midwives soon sparked into action and with some apprehension, given their initial error of thinking there was only one baby, helped my mother birth another baby. Except for one doctor, no one had indicated in the thirty-two weeks of my mother's pregnancy that she might be carrying more than one baby, but at 8 o'clock in the morning on December 8th, 1972, I was born. I had been lying in a breached position, so it wasn't an easy birth, and although I cried immediately after being born, I later stopped breathing for a while, which was of some concern.

I weighed 3lbs and 4oz and needed to be in special care and within an incubator. There was only one incubator in the vicinity, so I was rushed to intensive care to be looked after. Pippa joined me later so that we could be in the same place. My father soon joined my mother at the hospital. The doctors held little hope for our survival and quickly arranged for a vicar to come and christen us. Of course, my parents hadn't even thought of a name for me; they weren't expecting two babies. They quickly decided on Suzie Amanda. Pippa and I then began the fight for our lives, secured in an incubator.

We were medically termed as being 'Very Seriously Ill' (VSI), which is the military medical terminology for a patient who is 'very seriously ill and his or her illness is of such severity that life is imminently endangered'.

To the doctor's amazement, we kept up the fight, and the doctors took our names off the VSI list a month later. My mother first held us on January 7th, and she gave me my first feed a week later. I went home first, at the end of January, and the consultants finally discharged Pippa from the hospital three weeks later.

Those months that Pippa and I were in hospital must have been tremendously difficult for my parents. There was no telephone and all calls had to be booked through the camp. All the worry and the travelling the forty-five minutes back and forth to the hospital. However, they always remained positive, and they tell me they had no doubt we would pull through. Apparently, I fed well and gained good weight, and Pippa was very naughty and clever because she kept taking her feeding tube out of her nose! The hardest part for my parents was the lack of physical contact with their babies. The incubators were keeping us alive, and we had to spend all our time in there, a replication of a womb, but it meant that my mother could not enjoy that closeness with her babies, comforting us when we cried, feeding us, taking us out for a walk in those early days, holding us. However, the staff in the military hospital, and the care that they gave us, kept us alive.

After Pips and I were born, we remained under the care of the chief paediatrician at Rinteln. My parents tell me he was a nice man, and on our return to the United Kingdom, he organised all the appointments that I would need at the Military Hospital in Aldershot.

Soon after I came home, following my birth, my mother noticed that I had very stiff legs and they tended to settle in a scissor position. It was a real cause for concern for many months, so when we were back in the UK, the medical professionals at Cambridge Military Hospital in Aldershot referred me to Great Ormond Street hospital, where I came under the care of a paediatric orthopaedic surgeon, called Mr Fixsen. He was regarded as one of the foremost paediatric orthopaedic surgeons of his generation. I was very lucky to have him as my consultant, and he was instrumental in ensuring I had expert care from the very beginning. He offered opportunities for operations and physiotherapy that would ultimately help hugely with the impact that cerebral palsy was having on me. He was also a very nice, kind and gentle man with a fascinating career history. We had our first appointment with Mr Fixsen at Great Ormond Street hospital just after I was a year old.

Although my parents were obviously worried about my physical development and the various referrals, there had been no indication that I had any serious or long-lasting issues. It wasn't until about six months later, during a physiotherapy session, that the physiotherapist gave my mother a book on cerebral palsy and was told to prepare herself for me being wheelchair-bound for the rest of my life, unable to talk and probably incontinent.

This must have been shocking news for my parents, and utterly heartbreaking. It no doubt took some time to absorb what the specialists were saying and to accept the realisation that life would be different for my family and me. However, in the same way that my parents always believed we would defy the odds of survival at birth, they quickly adopted a positive frame of mind upon learning that I had cerebral palsy. They made a commitment to work closely with the specialists, to give me every chance of walking and leading a normal life.

I continued to have regular physiotherapy, endorsed by Mr Fixsen. The doctors suggested a specific approach to physiotherapy, called the Bobath principle. This is a form of therapy that draws upon occupational therapy, physiotherapy, and speech and language therapy. What was fundamentally different about this type of therapy is that it adopted a holistic approach; it was a lifestyle, rather than a session that I went to every day or a few times a week. My whole family embraced it and helped my mother incorporate it into our everyday life. I was encouraged to use the existing equipment that we had in the house, rather than the somewhat frightening paraphernalia of physiotherapy such as hoists and wheelchairs. However, it did mean my parents had to arrange the furniture in the house for my practical use, rather than for the aesthetic look. My sisters also were involved and helped. I was never alone, and family life was no doubt a constant source of thinking and deciding how best to support my needs, but in a fun and loving way.

There are different types of cerebral palsy. The cerebral palsy that I have prevented normal development of my motor function. For me, it specifically presents itself as muscle tightness and joint stiffness, so I have significantly reduced mobility. I have also suffered from a mild stutter, and the squint that I had (also known as a lazy eye) was most likely a result of the cerebral palsy.

As much as people try to say that they understand what it is like for me to have cerebral palsy, it is very difficult for anyone to relate to a disability unless they themselves are in a similar situation with a lack of mobility and an element of constant pain. It is incredibly frustrating not being able to do things quickly, and I now have an element of pain daily. People can think they are empathising, but they probably do not really understand. The pain can be unbearable at times. In my latter years, I have taken to using 'deep-heat' to stop my joints from hurting.

I will always wonder what it is like to be able to walk for long distances without the aid of sticks. I did experience walking when I was younger without sticks because my parents would encourage me to walk unaided between the two of them. I also remember my grandfather encouraging me to do this for small distances in his sitting room. During this short time, I got the feeling of freedom, of what it was like to walk without sticks. Interestingly, my most prevalent dream is the one when I dream that I am walking or running or dancing. I would love to be able to dance without sticks! When I dream that I am running or dancing, I feel so free ... and then I wake up.

When I was younger, my challenges were different. I don't remember as much pain and I rarely used a wheelchair. My mother tells me that I absolutely refused to use a wheelchair and I would scream if there was any attempt to put me in there. So I was usually in a buggy, or my mother would end up carrying me. My parents were always mindful of checking whether I was experiencing pain, as at such a young age, I might not have been able to verbalise the sensations that I was feeling due to the cerebral palsy. The spasticity that accompanied cerebral palsy caused a lack of feeling for me, so when I went to the doctors, they would check my sensations by pricking my skin with a pin. There would normally be no reaction, although I often had pins and needles and sore knees, which was likely to be due to early arthritis that would come and go.

In my adult years, I began to rely on my wheelchair much more, as the cerebral palsy began to take more of a hold. I also stopped receiving regular physiotherapy, which didn't help. Being in a wheelchair made planning to go out quite a process; there is a lot of thought that goes on in my head before I even leave, as I'm sure is the same for anyone else in a wheelchair due to age or disability. One of my first thoughts is, does where I am going have a disabled loo? Are there ramps, and not steps? Is there enough room to fit my wheelchair? And then can I get out of my wheelchair and use my sticks to move around? If I find that these adaptions aren't there, it just highlights my disability to me and makes me feel awkward and uncomfortable for those trying to help me and those that I have gone out with. It makes me feel as if I'm the one being awkward and difficult because I blame my legs for not working properly. I hate it; and at times, it has made me wish I had never ventured out. This is why it's so important that places do account for people in wheelchairs. Public places have improved significantly in the last ten years due to new regulations, but it wasn't always this way.

So, going to places that are not disabled-friendly is when the real frustration hits me, and then I sometimes cry inside because I can't manage it. I realise then I am disabled, and that it will always be this way.

The other major area of organising a trip out is time planning because I am not as speedy as everyone else, so I must allow myself plenty of time. I find the speed issue a real problem and it can exasperate me at times. I nearly can't explain, or put into words, how frustrated I get. I have always wanted to be quicker, but I physically can't. I would love to run. I could do a running circuit in my chair, but I know it wouldn't give me the same satisfaction of achievement that it would get if I walked that same circuit.

There was a time when my younger sister, Rosie, fractured her ankle and was on crutches for a couple of weeks. We talked about it and how hard she found it to use the crutches to walk and how tired she became after short distances, whereas when she could walk normally, she would have covered these distances with ease. So, she could relate to me for a short while, and I can very much relate to other people when they tell me that their joints hurt, for whatever reasons. However, I have no rest from pain at all, which I think can be difficult for other people to understand or appreciate. The difference is, when an able-bodied person is injured, has a limp, or finds themselves on crutches, they can bear their weight on the other leg. I am unable to do this because the cerebral palsy affects both of my legs.

When I am asked, 'How does cerebral palsy affect me on a daily basis?' I explain that I must do regular exercises to keep my legs from becoming too stiff. If I don't move my legs regularly enough, the circulation decreases, my legs become stiff, and so I would drag my legs when I walk. All of this just intensifies the pain and can cause my legs to spasm more frequently. There is also the obvious way that it affects me; I need to use two sticks to walk, and at other times, I need to use a wheelchair. I can't lie and say it doesn't frustrate me because it does, but there are always people worse off than me and that's what I must remember.

In the early days of living with cerebral palsy, I had two major operations in order to try to help with my ability to walk. I remember them well; I was so thankful for the opportunity to improve my walking, but the operations also came with a sense of anxiety for me.

The first operation was when I was six years old, and it was to rectify the scissor position of my legs. In this position, I could barely open them, and I could only walk on my toes. This operation was to manipulate four of my tendons to release my legs from the scissor position and to enable me to walk on my feet. The doctors had initially suggested that I have two separate operations to make these adjustments in my legs; two tendons at a time, but my parents were keen for me to only have the one operation to get this done, to minimise the number of times that I had to go through surgery, and to avoid me having such invasive operations when I was older and more physically mature. Thankfully, the doctors agreed that I could have all four tendons done in the one operation.

When the big day of my operation finally arrived, I felt quite scared. However, my mother and Rosie were with me, and the nurses were amazing, so I stayed strong and got through it. It must have been heartbreaking for my mother to see me in pain and such discomfort, but she held me close and told me that it was all going to be okay.

When I woke up in recovery, I wondered why I couldn't move. It felt as if a tonne of bricks had fallen on me. There was plaster covering the full length of both of my legs, and there were two bars going across the plaster from one leg to the other. This is a broomstick plaster. The purpose of the broomstick plaster was to keep the legs apart and the hip joint in a good position, and to prevent my legs from returning to the scissor shape. It was excruciatingly painful. I had to be in plaster for six to eight weeks. Even though I was only six, I remember it clearly.

Initially, I needed twenty-four-hour care, mainly to manage the pain. My mother stayed with me for the first few nights to help with the nursing. The hospital was well-equipped for my situation, so once the pain was under control, I was able to move around a bit and continue with my education, as the hospital had a small school attached to it.

I really didn't like staying in bed all day, so the hospital came up with an idea for me to get around. They gave me a wooden trolley. I thought it was fantastic! I pushed with my hands, whilst sitting in a wheelchair, and I felt so free. I didn't like it when I had to return to my bed.

My mother continued to help with my care and would often bring my youngest sister with her, Rosie, who was just eighteen months at the time. I remember Rosie making me laugh when she was in the cot, by making funny noises and popping up and shouting 'Boo'.

I have always loved music and during the times in hospital, I loved listening to the hospital radio. I remember trying to sing 'How much is that doggy in the window – I do hope the doggy is for sale'. It's funny how certain songs stick with you throughout your life. If I hear this song, I will always think of this time in hospital, having my first operation.

When the time came for me to have the plaster off, I was very scared. I remember a saw cutting through the very thick plaster. It tickled! Then without the plaster, my legs felt like feathers. However, it wasn't long before the pain began. It was like very bad pins and needles, constantly, and then my legs suddenly developed a mind of their own and went into spasm. I had no control over them, and it was painful. Eventually, the pain calmed down, but it would start again throughout the day for several weeks until I got used to moving my legs properly.

I had lots of physiotherapy after the operation, which helped me get some mobility back. I was now under the care of Mr Leonard, who had been recommended by Mr Fixsen and who was also admired by Mr Fixsen. Mr Leonard rightly explained that physiotherapy was more than walking. It was about exercising the relevant muscles in a particular and appropriate way, to try to remedy the problem that exists with them.

The doctors told me that I would need more operations later in my life, but following the first operation, I just concentrated on keeping mobile and following Mr Leonard and Mr Fixsen's advice.

When I was fourteen, I had another operation to lengthen and loosen my hamstrings. Before this operation, I couldn't straighten my knees, so having this operation allowed me to stand taller, stopped my legs from being so bent and enabled me to walk unaided in small spaces and for short periods of time. However, the operation also resulted in me finding it difficult to bend my knees, following them being straightened, so I again had extensive physiotherapy to give me exercises to help me loosen the legs a little. Physiotherapy is very intense; although it is for the greater good, it is not comfortable at all. I often called it 'the torture chamber'.

My biggest fear after any operation is the pain. My legs would have been in plaster for up to six weeks, so when the plaster came off, my legs would spasm and this was so painful. It is like having chronic pins and needles that don't go away. But I had been told that progressive physiotherapy was a way to manage any ongoing pain and mobility problems. I have continued to use exercise to keep my legs supple and to maintain movement; otherwise, they have a tendency to get very stiff.

When I was thirty-two years old, I completed a swimming marathon. I really committed to the training. It wasn't easy, but I got into a routine of going to the swimming pool every day. I primarily used my arms for swimming, because my legs didn't move very much, and I would alternate between swimming on my back and on my front; I probably couldn't have completed the marathon just on my front. Swimming on my back just gave me that rest between lengths because it was slightly easier.

I felt so free when I swam. I also felt like I was more like everyone else when I was in the water because in the water, I could walk just like everyone else! I could never understand why

I could walk in the water but not on land. I suppose it's having the weight taken off your legs which allowed them to move more freely. I used to fantasize that the whole world might one day be in a swimming pool, then I would have the best of both worlds; I would be able to walk and be like everyone else, whilst also being able to exercise like everyone else.

To complete the marathon was a major achievement for me. I couldn't have done it without all the training, and it was this determination that kept me going, knowing that I was going to reach a goal that I had set myself. I had a lot of encouragement from my family and friends, which helped so much. The staff at the swimming pool were also supportive, ensuring I had a lane to myself for the actual event. Pips was with me as I swam the marathon, giving me encouragement and praise. It meant so much to have her by the poolside, by my side, spurring me on.

On my last length, I suddenly saw a mass of people and this camera appeared. My eyesight was very blurry by this point, so I thought maybe I was seeing double! I wasn't! Unbeknown to me, Pips had arranged for the local newspaper to meet me at the end of the marathon. There they were, taking photos! They waited for me to get my breath back before briefly interviewing me. I was so touched that Pips had arranged this for me.

They went on to put an article together of my achievement. They also helped to promote the charity SCOPE that I was raising money for. SCOPE is a national disability charity that provides support and direct services to disabled people, along with campaigning to change the attitude towards people with disabilities. A group of parents and social workers, with disabled children of their own, founded it in 1952. The charity helps to ensure that disabled people receive the same rights to a good education and employment.

The text from the paper article was this:

> **Suzie Gets in the Swim for Charity**
>
> *Keen swimmer Suzie Dru Drury raises a smile after completing a marathon of 150 lengths of the staff pool at Salisbury District Hospital, the equivalent of swimming 3000 metres. Suzie, who lives in Wilton, is 32 and has cerebral palsy, which makes her sponsored swim even more remarkable because she does not have the use of her legs. She has visited the pool every day for the last three years, spending up to two hours swimming, finding that it helps her exercise as well as being a good way to lose weight. Suz decided to swim in aid of the cerebral palsy trust, SCOPE, and completed her marathon on Saturday, in just over two hours.*

Although it is one big frustration living with cerebral palsy, I don't like to complain about it all the time, because there's nothing anyone can do, and I don't want to sound miserable! However, it really isn't easy, and I have had to contend with a great deal over the years. I have learnt to live with it, and through it all, I have kept a personality and a sense of humour, which I hope will inspire other people to keep that 'spark' going in their own life. I also hope that people will always be grateful for their mobility. Completing the swimming marathon was one way for me to show that I can also push myself and focus on a goal and an achievement in the same way that anyone else can.

My family always keeps my spirits up if I do begin to feel low about living with cerebral palsy. There is one occasion that always makes me laugh when I think of it. I remember being in a green wheelchair (it is interesting how we remember the detail of some situations), and someone started talking to one of my sisters, about me. They couldn't seem to look at me, or didn't think to look at me, maybe because I reached their waistline rather than their eye line! They asked my sister a question about me; to which my sister replied, 'My sister can talk, you know. It's her legs that don't work, not her mouth!'

There were times when I did find people so patronizing, and this, again, is frustrating. However, on this occasion, my sister stood bold and literally said it as it was!

When I was younger, I used to think that I was the only one in the world who needed sticks to be able to walk. I was always around my family, who could all walk, so at this young age, I could never work out why I couldn't walk and everyone else could. Then I started school and I realised that there were many other children my age, some with similar disabilities, some with less of a disability, and some with far greater problems than my own.

During my school years, I did some travelling with the family. Seeing different people and going to new places also made me realise that I wasn't the only one who had physical difficulties. Travelling was always an experience for me; adapting to a new environment, keeping up with my siblings, contending with different accommodation, but we did it together as a family and we always had fun! I'll tell you more, but not before including a poem that I wrote about my disability, which I think makes me unique, in a way that only a disability can.

Unique DD

Cerebral palsy is in me, it's a lack of oxygen you see
It happens at birth when you first arrive on this earth
My brain feels like it's playing a game
But I wish my legs would stop being in pain
It drives me insane, but at times it has brought me some fame
In the things I do people recognise me too
It can't all be bad, so I'll not be sad
But at times it can feel like it's becoming so unreal.

I often wonder what it's like to walk
I am lucky enough to be able to talk
Lots of people are worse off than me, I forget that you see
Which is naughty of me, understanding one another is surely the key.

Day to day tasks can be challenging for me
In inaccessible places I can't wheel free
But people do offer their hands to me
And take me for a cup of flavoured tea
I think this is lovely jubbly and fits in with me splendidly.

My muscles don't relax
All they want to do is react
When people walk by they want to fly
And it's hard to control, I'm sure they do it for show
But I wish they would just go with the flow
It wouldn't be so embarrassing for me
I guess people realize it's just part of me.

Chapter 4

Travelling

Family life was busy, but fun! Rosie, my youngest sister, made a surprise appearance just under four years after Pippa and I were born. My parents had already dealt with the unexpected; twins and a daughter with special needs, so I'm sure their life was already challenging, giving them more than enough to contend with. Again, it was all against the odds. Despite taking precautions, they found themselves with another child on the way, another sibling for their three daughters. It must have been a trying time for my parents, and the suggestion of not continuing the pregnancy was presented to them, but this wasn't an option for my parents. They felt there was a reason for the pregnancy, and with the positivity they had so often drawn upon, the pregnancy went ahead, and Rosie was born a few months before our fourth birthday. We were now a family of six, Pippa and me only eleven months younger than Jenny, and now Rosie, four years younger than us. A family complete and unexpected, but totally embraced by my parents.

We were often on the move due to my father being in the army. I have lived in many different places, which has sometimes been challenging for me and my parents due to my disability.

The first week was always the hardest, working out how to use the stairs and get in and out of the bath, and how to just generally move around easily. It would take a while to establish exactly what I could and couldn't do, but it has also been a wonderful experience living in so many places, and I feel privileged to have had so many opportunities to see and live, in various locations, the most exotic place being Zimbabwe.

It's amazing how a mood can change when the word 'holiday' or 'travel' is mentioned. Getting ready for a holiday is exciting; all the organising, packing and anticipation. Getting ready for work certainly doesn't have the same lift! I love holidays and I seem to 'chill out to the max'. I have been on a few in my life, both abroad and within the UK.

When I was younger, our parents took us on three different narrowboat holidays, each lasting a week. Our first was on the River Thames in 1979, then the Stratford Canal in 1980, and our last was on the Lancaster Canal in 1982.

I loved our narrowboat holidays, although I did find it difficult to walk and move around the canal boat. My father always helped me on and off the boat. We had to walk along a gangplank, which is a flat and small, movable structure, akin to a bridge, which helped us to get from the land to the boat. This was not my strongest point because my balance was awful. I would have had a free bath if I had fallen in! The boat also had a little kitchen, and another small area for a table and chairs, then further into the boat, there were bunk beds. It was always fun to listen to my sisters say 'Bagsy the top bunk'. For obvious reasons I always slept on the bottom.

During the day, we used to park the narrowboat and explore different places near the canal. This was always good fun. I was just glad my family didn't rely on me for any directions; we could have ended up in Timbuktu if they had! Luckily, my father was fully in control and had the day mapped out and planned for us. I was fascinated when we moved through the canal locks, watching how they locked and unlocked. I could tell you needed to be strong to do this whole process, and if you didn't have the strength at the beginning, you would have certainly gained it by the end! I watched upon my sisters sometimes helping my father; I liked to think that I supported them all from the side-line.

I loved it when we went through the tunnels; you could hear all the echoes when we spoke. My sisters and I used to see whose echo would last the longest. That was good fun. Although I often got a sore throat from shouting so much, maybe that was a blessing in disguise for everyone. It certainly kept me quiet for a while.

There was a thunderstorm during one of our narrowboat holidays. This made it quite exciting, counting the claps of thunder and seeing the strikes of lightning, all whilst watching Chitty Chitty Bang Bang, until the television signal gave up due to the weather.

On the last narrowboat holiday, Rose was the only one who avoided the dreaded chickenpox. Jen, Pips and I were itching for England and went through a mountain of calamine lotion. We consoled ourselves that at least it was the end of the holiday and not at the beginning. We all slept on the way home in the back of our green Hillman Hunter Estate car, called 'Greenbella'.

Another of our memorable family holidays was a week that we spent on the Isle de Oleron, in France, during the summer of 1983. We stayed in a beautiful, modern bungalow. Every morning my sisters and I would walk up to the local baker to collect some fresh bread. There was an air of excitement as we practised the French pronunciation for 'Please can I have a loaf of bread' on the way to the shop. When we got there, I would savour the smell of freshly made bread and wonder how I would ever be able to walk back to the bungalow without eating it. The walk to and from the bakery was a good challenge for me; I tried to keep up. I was certainly ready for my breakfast when we got back!

The weather was warm in France at that time of year, and we spent many days on the beach. I found it difficult to walk on the sand with the tripod sticks that I had at the time, so my father would carry me on his shoulders. I'm sure it made the walk quicker because no one had to wait for me, but I'm not sure how easy it was for him. His only request was that I didn't talk too much! Every time I talked, my whole body would tense up, especially my legs, which would then shoot out. So, I can now see how this must have made it particularly difficult for my father when he was carrying me. Walking along the sand, carrying a child on your shoulders is hard enough without battling with a random foot in your face! It was quite hard for me too, though, as I found it so difficult to keep quiet. I remember quite a few giggles as my father teased me, saying, 'Stop talking, Suz!' as we soldiered on down the beach, me with the best view.

I loved watching my sisters run into the sea, trying to skip the waves. They would swim quite far out. I was always worried that they didn't know where to stop, how far they should go, but they always returned safely. I tried swimming in the sea but found it difficult because the bottom of the sea was very uneven, which made it hard for me to balance. I could never get my footing. When I did try, when I finally got my balance, the waves would come in strong, crashing in around me, catching me off guard and instantly knocking me and my tripod, or sticks, over. In a swimming pool, however, I could stand, so it was easier, and there was even a handrail if I needed it.

France was the place where I discovered flavoured chewing gum. What a novelty! My sisters and I loved trying all the different tastes. However, when I admitted that I actually swallowed the chewing gum, wild and worried faces greeted me, telling me, 'No, you must never swallow chewing gum!'

'It can get tangled up in your insides,' my eldest sister proclaimed.

Well, that delayed me getting to sleep for a few nights, imagining chewing gum that I had already swallowed getting tangled up inside of me. From then on, I promptly put the chewing gum in the bin, as soon as I had chewed it enough.

It was lovely to all be together on a family holiday. It was also educational too, understanding how the locks worked on the narrowboat holidays and practising how to order a French loaf of bread whilst we were in France. But I must admit to sometimes wishing I could have been as physically abled as my sisters were, especially on the narrowboat holidays, when they were helping with opening and closing the locks. However, in hindsight, we could still be there now if they had left it to me!

Then came our ultimate holiday and the phenomenal opportunity to live in Zimbabwe, in the capital, Harare. My parents accepted a posting there by the army in 1984, for three years. By this time, my sisters and I had settled into boarding school, so we flew out to Zimbabwe for the holidays; three times a year. Christmas, Easter and the long summer holidays, which was the winter season in Africa.

The reason for the posting to Zimbabwe was (in brief) to help with the unification of the three Zimbabwean forces (Mugabe's, Nkumo's and Smith's) who had been fighting. The intention was to make them a combined army. My father's job was to help oversee this unification. He taught the army's senior officers how to command their army but then set up a unique tactical trainer so they could practice their command skills without having to have troops on the ground.

My father's work in Zimbabwe was one of many deployments. Earlier in his career, during a posting in Chertsey, he was awarded an MBE for his work on deploying the army in the UK. It must have been a proud moment for my mother and him when he received his medal from her Majesty the Queen.

Zimbabwe was a real privilege to experience. The army had given us, as a family, a unique opportunity to live abroad. My sisters and I were at different boarding schools, so our term times were never the same. Thankfully, negotiations between parents and schools meant that we did manage to leave schools at the same time so that even though we might have missed a week or two of the end of term, we could all still travel out to see our parents and our home, together. However, the headmaster of my school wasn't forgiving and insisted that I undertook a project during my holiday and reported it back to school when I returned. So much for some time off schoolwork for me!

When we were on our school holidays in Zimbabwe, we used to travel around. We went to Victoria Falls, a memory I will savour. It was amazing! We took a boat down the Zambezi, watching the sunset and the wildlife settle down in the evening sun to their place of rest for the night. We also stayed in a beautiful holiday lodge at the Lake Mcilwaine. We were reminded of the beauty of living in Africa when, as we arrived and were unpacking our food, we noticed some monkeys hanging out in the nearby trees. They obviously saw the bananas that we had brought with us and decided that these would be very nice for their own lunch. They promptly came swinging into our kitchen and stole them from right under our nose!

I also have fond memories of horse riding when on our school holidays in Zimbabwe. There was a riding school called Max's Riding School, which was very close to our house. My mother took us all there regularly for horse riding lessons. We were there so often we began to feel like part of the yard! Maybe less of a fond memory was the time that I was enjoying a ride on one of the horses, but it then decided to increase its speed to a trot, and then to a canter ... after which I fell off. Thankfully uninjured!

Travelling to Zimbabwe three times a year equated to six flights a year. So, all that travelling back and forth certainly got me used to flying. The flight from Heathrow or Gatwick to Zimbabwe was a long nine and half hours. Our grandfather used to take us to the airport. He always gave us sweets for the flight so our ears wouldn't feel blocked or pop with the change of cabin pressure.

On arrival at the airport, a porter would thankfully bring me a wheelchair. We all breathed a sigh of relief at this point, as we knew that otherwise my sisters and I would have missed the flight, waiting for me to walk to the departures lounge. The airport porters were very helpful. I remember I had to go through a different part of customs to my sisters because of my wheelchair. I used to dread this. The authorities would search me, and I never quite understood why, but it always happened. We then waited in the departures lounge until our flight was called, so 'all was good in the hood' in the end.

We had a 'nanny' who was assigned to us to look after us during the flight. Due to our young age, we were classed as unaccompanied minors, which meant we needed to have an adult to look after us during the flight. About ten minutes before everyone was due to board, the nanny would escort my sisters and me onto the aeroplane so that I could settle before the chaos began. Everyone was so helpful to me; I couldn't have done it on my own.

The nine-and-a-half-hour flight was tiring for me even though I wasn't doing much. My legs got incredibly stiff, and I couldn't get up and walk around like other people did. I felt I burdened my sisters because when I did need to get up, I needed their help. One of them would always come with me. To steady myself when walking down the aisle, I had to hold onto the seats as I passed. As much as I tried not to, I was swaying all over the place. Thank goodness for one of my sisters giving me support.

On one occasion, I remember a chap, joking with us, who said, 'Oh, have you had a few drinks?'

'No,' I said, feeling irritated.

Pips, who was helping me on this occasion, was quick to stick up for me and said, 'My twin sister has cerebral palsy. Leave her alone!'

The look on this person's face was a picture!

It always amused me that as soon as I finally got out of my seat to make the trek down the aisle to the bathroom, the seatbelt sign would suddenly go on. It was always at the most inconvenient time, and I had no choice but to return immediately to my seat. Back down the aisle, swaying. I decided it was better if I just stayed in one place.

Eating on the aeroplane was another interesting experience for me. I don't think it's that easy for the most able-bodied people, but it certainly challenged me more than others! I kept shaking so the food invariably ended up on my lap, or the floor, and never really reached my mouth. Having a drink was even harder – that just tended to go everywhere. The situation would be drastically exacerbated should someone nearby cough or sneeze, or should an announcement be made, because then, of course, my body would immediately resort to an involuntary response so that I would jump and spill the entire drink. There was never a dull moment for any of us during these flights!

Being young and unaccompanied minors on such a long flight meant that the cabin crew often gave us some special attention, so we felt as comfortable and relaxed as possible. On one flight, they invited us to see the cockpit. This was amazing, seeing all the controls and talking to the pilots about how they flew the aeroplane. Interestingly though, it didn't make me want to take up flying lessons; to be honest, I can hardly find my way home, yet alone take to the sky.

We really were spoilt and very well looked after, which made flying on our own a much more exciting experience. When our flight landed in Harare, our nanny gave us a bag of chocolates and sweets.

My sisters and I were literally buzzing the moment that we arrived at Harare, the capital of Zimbabwe. It was always strange landing in such warmth and sunshine, having left a country only twelve hours previously where rain prevailed, or sometimes snow.

It was wonderful to see the sun! However, it did take us a little while to adjust and we took the time to chatter endlessly to our parents, catching up on all the news.

We had a guard dog when we lived in Zimbabwe, called 'Shumba'. Shumba means lion in the local dialect, Shona. He was a Rhodesian Ridgeback, which is a known breed able to kill lions, due to their size and ferocity. Shumba was no exception; he was a big dog, probably a similar size to a Great Dane, but for some reason, he didn't have the ferocity that was expected of such breeds. People usually bought them to be guard dogs for their house, but Shumba was a sensitive dog, very gentle and placid, and although he looked scary and would probably ward off any burglars just by his size, look and bark, I'm not sure how effective he would have been had the burglars shown him some love and attention! I did feel protected by him, and it felt as if he understood me on a level that was different from how humans understood me. He didn't like walking on shiny floors, which was awkward because our kitchen had a shiny floor, so for this reason he chose not to come inside. His little house was a kennel on the veranda. I understood his fear of shiny floors because I didn't like them either. They often caused me to slip and slide and eventually fall over if my sticks didn't quickly give me the support I needed at the time. Shumba and I became firm friends.

One day my mother came home with four Rhodesian Ridgeback puppies! We couldn't believe our luck and Shumba finally had some fellow four-legged creatures to fuss over. The puppies weren't for us to keep; we were just looking after them and trying to sell them, whilst their owner (my mother's hairdresser!) was away. How convenient that there were four of them. We had one each. Jenny named hers Big Boy, Pippa called her puppy Big Ears, and Rosie chose the name Big Feet for her puppy. I called my puppy Casper.

My father made some kennels out in the garden. Every morning we would rush out to see the puppies, say good morning and give them their food. We would play with them all day and leave it as long as possible before saying goodnight to them. It was heartbreaking when people came to visit and decided to take one away with them. Big boy, the most boisterous, was the first to go, followed by Big Ears, and then Big Feet.

Casper suffered from epilepsy and was very sensitive and timid. We all grew fond of him, maybe because of his vulnerability, but also because he was so gentle and affectionate. We had other potential buyers coming to see him, but no one wanted a sensitive Rhodesian guard dog who wasn't showing the ferocity required to protect a home. Eventually, we decided to keep him. He came home with us when we returned to the UK and went on to live a full happy eight years with us. He was a special dog. My sister Rosie remembers the day that my father went off in the car to collect Casper from kennels, following a family holiday in Formentera. She remembers feeling devastated as she looked out of the window awaiting Casper's return, only to see my father come back empty-handed. Casper had died in the kennels whilst we were away.

Living in Zimbabwe was a completely different way of life, and I am so grateful to have experienced it. I'm sure my sisters would agree. The Africans were so friendly, always willing to help, and always with a smile. A local family helped with our cleaning and gardening. Generie would come over daily to clean, iron and tidy our rooms. Generie lived with Alfred and Lovemore, who were brothers. They both helped with the gardening. Generie had a little boy called Charles. They had very basic accommodation at the bottom of our garden and would cook in the open on a fire made of wood. They did not have any electricity but my father felt that this was not good enough, and so he ran an electric cable to them which gave them lighting and something to cook on. We used to quiz them daily about how to say, 'good morning', 'good afternoon', or 'good evening' so that we could greet them or say goodbye to them at the end of the day, using their language. 'Mangwanani akanaka', Masikati akanaka' or 'Manheru akanaka'.

Our house in Zimbabwe was wonderful. Big, with lots of land and several verandas. We also had a swimming pool. This was perfect for me as it allowed me to keep up the exercise and it was a form of physio. I tried to swim as many as eight times a day. Never on my own and always with armbands, until one day I forgot to put the armbands on but managed to swim without them!

This gave me such a feeling of freedom. It felt as if for once, I could keep up with my sisters. I describe it as an 'off the hook' feeling. If only I could have done this on land. However, this was never to be, unless I was charging around in my wheelchair, or on 'my pony' (which was like an electric scooter) because my sisters could rarely keep up with that!

In the swimming pool, I tried to do sitting dives to improve my swimming technique, but they always ended up as belly flops in a true 'Suz style'! My sisters and I also managed a few 'mushroom float' competitions. I used to hold my legs in a bent position then count how long I could stay underwater for and hope that it was longer than what my sisters could do. I enjoyed this, as it was easy to compete with them and I often came out as the winner.

We had a rubber tyre that we used to play on whilst in the pool. It's the only way I can describe it. It was black and it had a hole in the middle, just like a black rubber tyre! My sisters and I used to share the time we had with the tyre, and when it was our turn, we would sit on it and glide up and down the pool. Naturally, I wanted to do everything that my sisters were doing so that I didn't feel left out. So when it was my turn, I grabbed hold of the tyre, put my legs through the big hole in the middle and eased myself from the side of the pool into the water; just as I had seen my sisters do. Unfortunately, the tyre ring then proceeded to somehow flip over me, leaving me head down in the water, unable to recover from the situation. Jenny, my eldest sister, came to the rescue and eased me out of my potentially fatal predicament. My parents had always been very strict about how we were never, ever to swim alone. I now understood why! I also learnt that I should not try to copy other people, particularly able-bodied people, without understanding the extent of my own ability first.

This event gave me a scare, but it did not perturb me from the swimming pool. I wanted to swim all the time, even when it was raining. Sometimes my sisters would join me, but I don't know if they had the same enthusiasm. They shuddered a bit at the idea of getting themselves cold and wet in the rain before jumping into a pool. But for me, the lure of the water, the promise that I could submerge myself into a pool that took away the pain and allowed me to move in a way that I couldn't do when I was walking, was just too much to resist.

One afternoon we were all by the pool and suddenly we heard thunder. In Zimbabwe the thunder would rumble in from nowhere, bulldozing across the skies with no warning. In the same way, the sky taps would just open and rain would pour. There was no quick look on an app to check out the weather in those days. As the thunder boomed and the rain expelled from the thick clouds above, my sisters took to their feet and darted back to the house probably in a flash that was quicker than the expectant lightning. I must admit, my first thought was 'charming'. Leaving me here, by the water, during a thunderstorm, on my own. I willed my legs to move faster as I tried to make the treacherous journey back to the house, and then, in the distance, I saw Generie. She came to my rescue and carried me back to the house. So, I got there in the end and I live to tell the tale!

We had a long driveway that led down to our house. The drive curved around and down past the tennis court and then past the swimming pool which was set slightly further back from the tennis court. It was a stony drive, so my parents always drove slowly down it and my sisters had to cycle even more slowly to save themselves riding over a random large stone, stealthily protruding from the collection, and promising to throw them off their bike. This was frustrating for them as I knew that they wanted to hurtle down as fast as they could, making the most of the hill.

The route of our driveway ended in a spacious stony area, where my parents parked the cars in the nearby garage, where my sisters kept their bikes, and where I kept 'my pony' (the electrical scooter) that I had. We all had fun times on the pony; I would let my sisters drive around on it too.

To get from the driveway to the house, there were several steps to climb. When we first moved into the house and I saw these steps, I realised I was going to have to tackle this head-on! After some family discussion and help from my parents, I discovered that rather than attempting to climb the steps foot after foot, the best method was sitting down on each step and lifting myself up to the next step, using my arms. My arms were getting increasingly stronger from all the swimming that I was doing, which helped. This proved to be the best option, and there were times that I even raced, and beat, my sisters up the steps.

My sisters never made it easy though! Particularly my younger sister, Rosie. She used to play this game where she would creep up on me and then hide behind a bush, tree, door, whatever would hide her, and then leap out and shout 'Boo' directly at me. It would make me jump and we would all laugh. I was pleased though that my sisters didn't single me out or treat me any differently because of my disability. I wanted to be like them and try to do all the things that they were doing.

The verandas were a significant part of our house, offering a place of solitude, a place of peace; somewhere to escape to if you wanted to just sit in silence and hear the sound of the crickets and nature talking to each other. I often found my mother doing just this on one of the verandas when we had busied ourselves playing elsewhere. The verandas were what made the house unique; there was not just one, but three! We used to have our afternoon tea on the front veranda, and often our lunch and sometimes our breakfast. Pips used to make banana cake. It was lush and always our favourite. It would have certainly won her Master Chef if the programme were on at the time! We would enjoy slice after slice during teatime, sitting on the front veranda, looking out onto our long, escaping garden, which had six chickens at the end of it.

During the holidays we were always finding different ways to amuse ourselves. We didn't have the technological devices that children have nowadays to keep them busy and in touch with friends remotely. Keeping in touch with friends was only done by letter writing, and there would be quite a significant period between sending a letter and getting a reply. So, it really was down to me and my sisters to provide ourselves with that entertainment. I don't know whose idea it was, or whether there might have been a bit of encouragement from our parents, but someone suggested that we do a play. So, we decided to put on a performance of 'Toad of Toad Hall'. I was Mole, Jenny was Rat, Pippa was Toad, and Rosie was Badger. I don't remember it that well, but thankfully my father videoed our performance. It is so funny watching it back! We performed it out in the garden. I think we all did very well. I only forgot my lines once, Jenny waved at the camera when one of us made a mistake, so my father would stop filming. I think Pippa had her lines on a bit of paper nearby, the paper acting as a discarded newspaper that Toad was reading. Rosie took it a bit further and was reading her lines at one point, whilst pretending to read a book. Such fond memories of us as young sisters, all together, enjoying each other's company and making use of this phenomenal garden that we were so lucky to have in Zimbabwe. We spent most of our time in the garden as the weather was so warm.

When we weren't practising drama, sometimes I used to sit on the nearby bench and watch my sisters, and sometimes my parents, play tennis. As an onlooker, I was able to detect any cheating, and I soon discovered there was a bit of this going on. A call for 'that was definitely out', when I could see that it had completely hit within the line, meant that someone was usually trying to cheat! It was all good fun and I just let the game continue.

My youngest sister, Rosie, and I used to talk to each other in a made-up foreign language. Neither of us had a clue what we were talking about, but we pretended to understand. It was very funny! Sisters being sisters and passing some carefree time. Rosie sometimes called herself Doctor Wiggles (Wiggles was her nickname!) She used to make her room into a doctor's surgery, with a notice on the door, stating 'Dr Wiggles Doctor's Surgery'. You had to book an appointment and stick firmly to that time, and you had to knock before entering. I would then have to feign an illness, talk it through with her, and she would then ask me questions and take notes, then tell me what I needed to do. It was very well organized. Even her teddy bears got appointments!

We had some lovely neighbours in Zimbabwe. Well, although they were neighbours, we had to walk quite a way to see them, as our houses weren't that close together, with a great expanse of land separating them. Our garden in Zimbabwe stretched about four acres. We would often walk across to our closest neighbour, a lovely lady called Mrs Hummel. She used to give us a cup of tea and biscuits, and she also smoked a lot of cigarettes. She had a maid too. One day her maid brought us a pot of tea; we left it to brew, but then when we finally poured the tea from the pot, we realised she had forgotten to put the tea bags in! We laughed quite a lot about that!

Living in Zimbabwe was an opportunity of a lifetime, and we all have many happy memories, captured in many photo albums, which we love to look back on. The hardest part was leaving to go back to school and saying goodbye to our parents at the airport. However, we knew it wasn't long until we would be back on the plane, heading out to the African air, and the excitement would begin all over again. Going to school was a necessity, but having our holidays in Zimbabwe was a luxury.

Let me tell you more about school, which was a completely different chapter of my life, but not before I include my poem on 'The Travelling Bee'.

A Travelling Bee

A Travelling Bee, that's me
I have lived abroad
This I adored and never got bored
Africa was the place to be
With many places to see
It was educational for me
This helped me with my Geography
And projects that people liked to see
I loved going on Safari
And seeing the animals run free.

I have visited Victoria Falls
I've never seen anything so remarkable before
It took my breath away for sure
As I watched the water fall
Into the Zambezi Gorge
I will always remember this forever more.

I swam every day
A water baby people might say
The insects wouldn't be far away
A hornet liked the taste of me one day
"Ouch" that's all I could say
My Father saved the day
By taking it away.

"The Dru Drury Crew" tried acting too
"Toad of Toad Hall" Father videoed us all
Sisterly love helped us through
We all remembered our lines
So there were no "Take Two's"
The sun stayed out too.

Moving around the UK
Had its perks too
Meeting different people
Who understood the upheaval
That we were going through
Of boxes everywhere and in storage too
Some people say "I wish I was as lucky as you
It all sounds so cool"

Chapter 5

School days

My first school was in Chertsey, a school called White Lodge, which was a centre of excellence for disabled children. I only went in once a week for a while, but I soon settled in, so the school then accepted me on a permanent basis. My parents arranged for me to have transport to and from the school. This helped my mother out, as she was busy getting Jenny and Pippa to school and it was a thirty-minute drive to White Lodge from our house in Shepperton. Logistically it would have probably been impossible for my mother to get us all to school on time, driving in different directions. However, during the early days of going to White Lodge, my mother made sure she took me, and she would often stay for the day to learn the ways that the staff were helping me so that she could do the same at home.

When I was going every day, a woman called Mary Ryan, who worked at the school, drove me to White Lodge each day. Mary also had cerebral palsy. I enjoyed spending time with Mary when she drove me into school. She was the first person to notice that I loved singing and that my voice wasn't too bad. Years later, at my next school, I used to stand up in assembly and sing a solo and everyone clapped when I had finished. I felt so proud. I still enjoy singing today. Mary also loved playing the guitar. I tried playing the guitar once and loved it too. My godmother bought me my first guitar. I was so happy and played it as often as I could. Unfortunately, I didn't keep the guitar-playing up, but I still love to listen to the sound of it now. I find it very relaxing. White Lodge was a good school, and my parents tell me they saw marked improvements in my walking and education whilst I was there because I had some specialist teaching and regular physiotherapy. I also met some nice people, who I met again at another school that I went to years later.

The army then posted my father to Catterick. This is the other side of the country to Shepperton, so we had to move house. It was always more difficult for my parents to arrange schooling for me than it was for them to arrange it for my sisters. They persisted with trying to keep me in a mainstream school as they felt it was important for me to be around able-bodied children. A school called Le Cateau in Catterick seemed to provide the best balance between a mainstream school and providing facilities and support for me. It already educated two disabled children. However, I didn't stay here for long. The school said that they struggled to cater for me and to provide the extra support that I needed. They claimed there was a health and safety problem with me being at the school, so they sent me home. My parents only found out that I was on my way home when the army medical officer called my mother to let her know that the school couldn't accommodate me. My parents were furious, and although my memory of this is vague, it must have been unsettling for me and incredibly worrying for my parents, who now had to find me another school.

The nearest specialist school was in Newcastle, called 'Percy Headley'. I would have to be a weekly boarder because it wasn't realistic to drive me there every day due to the distance. My parents agonised about whether to send me, but there seemed to be very little choice. I had to be educated, I needed specialist help and the local schools could not provide this.

Being part of an army family meant that we were going to be moving around on a regular basis. Not only was it common for children from army families to go to boarding school, but it was always the plan for us to have a private education eventually. Both my parents had been to boarding school so it felt very natural to give us the same opportunity. The military would also subsidise the fees, and it would give my sisters and me the security and consistency of a base whilst my parents inevitably moved around. It also meant that we received a stable syllabus which would help with our education.

Over the years my parents had thought long and hard about all the options around living an army life with four children who needed to be in education, and with me who needed specialist help. They had considered being apart from each other so that my father did the travelling and my mother settled in a house close to the schools so we could easily come home on weekends, but they just knew this wouldn't work for many reasons. They hadn't got married to then have to live apart. The travelling that my father might have to do was not predictable, and they had already spent much time apart during the early years of the army career. My father thought about coming out of the army; however, he was at the height of his career and enjoying it, and with a family of six to support, the idea of leaving the security of well-established employment just to reduce the need for travel would have been a big risk to take. Added to this, was the implication of a low economic climate, which it was at the time. Also, there were arguably bleak opportunities of work in the civilian world, so there was a chance my father would not get a stable or permanent job, giving him the equivalent salary; and as a large family, we just could not afford this. Therefore, boarding school in the long-term, with my father remaining in the army, seemed the most sensible option all around. My father had really enjoyed his time at boarding school, my mother less so. Therefore, I think my father was keener for us to go than my mother, but my mother could see that it was the best option to ensure stability and a good and consistent education.

The situation that my parents were in, with the problem of schooling me, was over forty years ago. In today's world, there is so much more emphasis on providing support to disabled children, and I don't think a school would be allowed to send a child home on the grounds of health and safety and being unable to support that child. There is the option of one-on-one care within schools now for children with special needs, and I believe that a primary school would make every effort to integrate a disabled child within their school, particularly as my problems weren't related to any learning difficulties; at the time it was purely associated with my physicals needs. The way Le Cateau School responded to me just wouldn't be acceptable today. It's interesting how times have changed.

I started at Percy Headley when I was six years old as a weekly boarder, which I loved. It was a very long drive for my mother when she came to pick me up, and she had to bring my sisters with her, and my youngest sister was only two years old, so I'm sure the travel wasn't very easy ... or relaxing! My father was away much of the time due to his job, so he wasn't able to help. It must have been hard for my mother, as any parent could appreciate; I know that she hated leaving me for the week. Apparently, I would scream and scream, but my mother was always reassured by the staff that I soon settled down once the week started, and I seemed happy.

I wasn't at Percy Hedley for long. I got very homesick and so I was pleased when we moved house, which meant that I had to leave. Towards the end of my time at this school, I had a particularly bad experience. It began with a leg spasm. My legs regularly go into spasm, which is frustrating. It's notably involuntary, so I don't know it's going to happen; it causes unwanted movement, and it is often painful. It is a result of incorrect signals from the brain. When the legs go into spasm they jerk forward; sometimes this can go in my favour if I'm talking to someone who is irritating me. However, on this occasion, at school, I was trying to reach for my slipper, and this was when my legs went into spasm. The result was that my leg was caught under a hot radiator pipe, and I couldn't move it. Staff soon came to my rescue when they heard me screaming.

The army posted my father back to the south, and we lived in Fleet, in Hampshire, for the next couple of years. I went to a mainstream infant school called Bagshot School. This was a school for able-bodied children, but it had a separate department for people with physical disabilities. I really liked being part of a school where there were other children my age who could walk and who didn't suffer from a disability. It allowed me, in some way, to forget about my own disability; I just concentrated on fitting in with my peers. I was only seven years old, so I was still making sense of the world and trying to understand my disability. I remember trying to run in the playground so I could be like all the other children, but of course, I soon realised that I couldn't run, or if I tried, I would end up on the floor! Again, I think I just forgot that I couldn't run. People were kind to me and made sure I was ok. After playtime, when we heard the whistle, we all had to line up and remain quiet. I found this particularly difficult. Keeping silent isn't a strong point of mine!

Sports day was always good fun. The egg & spoon race was one of my favourites. I found it hard to do, but I always gave it a go, although my egg usually ended up on the floor, and I never won, despite having a head start. Surely, it's the taking part that counts.

The next and final school that I went to was a boarding school called the Lord Mayor Treloar College in Alton. I was there for ten years, between 1981 and 1991. It was a prestigious school and one that catered to children with special needs, but it took children all through from primary to secondary education, so going here meant that I didn't have to change schools yet again when my primary school years finished. I think initially the finances were a concern for my parents. Treloars was of a very high standard and was recognised worldwide, so it wasn't cheap. My parents explored many ways to pay for this education. They spent much time and exchanged a few letters between both the county council and the army, who both could potentially offer funding. Eventually, as we were about to move to Weeton, in Lancashire, due to another posting from the army, the Lancashire local authorities agreed to pay all the fees and did so until I left.

Knowing what I know now about the situation that my parents were in at the time, I can see that they gave me the best solution possible under the circumstances. I was able to continue with my education in a secure and consistent environment, and in a place that would provide me with the best quality and specialist support in my development, within the confines of my disability. I was also living a similar life to my sisters, which has always been important to me. They too were at boarding school.

Treloars provided educational and occupational therapy, speech and language therapy together with independence and medical support to young people with disabilities from all over the UK and overseas. As a bit of background, the Treloar Trust, a registered charity, which also runs the sister institute Treloar College, supports and administers the Lord Mayor Treloar College. Sir William Purdie Treloar, the Lord Mayor of the city of London at the time, founded the school and it opened in 1908. Prior to its opening, Sir William had set up a fund as part of his mayoral appeal to help people who couldn't walk or move properly. His initial aim was to build a hospital and school outside the city, for children with non-pulmonary tuberculosis. Since it opened over a hundred years ago, Treloar's has steadily grown and has become one of the country's leading providers of education, care, therapy and medical support.

My father's second cousin, Kay, was so impressed with Treloars, with what it could offer me and with how it helped me over the years, that she donated a significant amount of money to the trust. As did a dear family friend, Marjorie Cave, who was married to a wonderful man who we called Mr Toffeeman, because he always gave us toffees. It was years later that my parents told me Kay and Marjorie donated these large sums of money, and it is a testament to how the school supported me, and others, during our primary and teenage years.

I was reluctant and a little scared to go to another boarding school because I hadn't liked being away from home when I was at Percy Headley. However, it had always been the intention for my sisters and me to be privately educated, as my parents were, and Treloars was one of the best boarding schools in the country for disabled people. I also could not have withstood the constant changing schools every time the army posted my father somewhere different, which was invariably every two years. It also wouldn't have been possible for me to be educated in Zimbabwe when we were posted there. The country had just ended a civil war, and my mother was one of the first wives allowed out there. Therefore, if my sisters and I hadn't been at boarding school, the only options for my parents were for either my mother to leave my father for three years, which would have broken our family up, or for my father to have not taken this opportunity. The posting came with some significant financial incentive and career prospects, which my father just could not, and should not have, said no to.

My mother took me to my first interview and stayed by my side. I was very scared but soon calmed down when I arrived. I met two fellow students on this day: Chris Piggott and Luke Wilson, both very nice. I remember sitting down for lunch and we had fruit salad for pudding, which I loved so I had a second helping (well, it's healthy), and I was subsequently called 'The Fruit Salad lady' because I liked it so much.

Before starting at Treloars, I did a second tour of the school. I remember thinking, 'Gosh, there are lots of people in wheelchairs'. I always thought that cerebral palsy was the only disability because that's all I had known before going to Treloars. I really couldn't understand why some people were in wheelchairs one day and not in wheelchairs on other days. Have they had a miracle overnight that has enabled them to walk? If so, where did this happen, and more importantly, would it work for me? It was a harsh reality when, as I grew up, I realised this just didn't happen.

When we had finished the assessment day, the wait began to find out if I had a place at the school or not. It was an anxious time for us all. We eventually got the news. I had a place at Treloar's. I had mixed emotions; I was sad because I knew I wouldn't see much of my parents or sisters during term time, but I was happy and relieved because I knew it was best for me and would provide me with so many opportunities that I really wouldn't get anywhere else. I wouldn't have to keep moving schools whenever my parents moved house, or missing school days due to a school not being able to accommodate me for certain activities. Treloars was especially adapted for disabled people; it had the right facilities and equipment, so it made everyday activities so much easier. It also had a physiotherapy department and a sickbay, so everything was on site. In that respect, I was lucky, and it was the right place for me.

My mother drove me to Treloars on a Sunday evening, so I would be ready to start school on the Monday. I was nervous as we turned into the driveway of the school, and it all suddenly became very real! Kate Framp, the unit leader, met me as we arrived, and she told me that I was in Gaston House, which was for younger pupils. Kate was nice and made me feel comfortable and at home straight away. At the lower school, there were three other houses. Pike House, Burnham and Jephson House. I was then shown to the dormitory where I was sharing with three other children who were also new to the school so at least we were probably all feeling the same mix of emotions. My mother helped me unpack and then we had to say our goodbyes. This was a very difficult moment for both of us.

I had a very strange first night. I kept waking up thinking I was still at home; I shed a few tears, which I think was very natural. The care staff would come and wake us up in the morning to make sure we were up in time for breakfast. We would all have to wait outside the dining room, in a line, in our appropriate houses. During the week, the house staff told us where to sit. Luckily, I was with a nice crowd of people and so it was fun. After breakfast, we had to go back to the house to get our school things and then it was off to assembly.

After assembly, we went to the classroom. I was in a class called J1. The teacher, Mrs Lydon, was nice. There were quite a few of us in this classroom, and I began to feel more at ease, especially when I recognised some faces from White Lodge, my very first school. Mrs Lydon asked where I would like to sit, so I was able to make sure that I sat with the people I knew. We all introduced ourselves. It was nerve-racking, but I managed it.

During one of the first lessons, Mrs Lydon said we were going to practice our timetables. I knew a few (thanks to my grandparents, who had practised them with me endlessly) and I was just praying that she would give a timetable that I knew. It must have been my lucky day because she asked me if I knew my seven times table, which I did. I got them all right too!

Time went by quite fast, which was good, and I soon started to settle into boarding school life. I made new friends and quite soon introduced myself to a girl named Sophie. We soon became close friends. We would always wait for one another at the end of classes. I knew instantly that we would be soul mates and we were!

Sophie became and remained my best friend throughout our school years. I could talk to her about anything, and she would always help me out. I had never had such a special friend. Sophie was like my sister and because I spent so much time with her, we became very close. Sophie's birthday is the 28th of November and mine is the 8th of December, so we often had a joint party, which was always great fun. It also meant that we shared the same star sign, Sagittarius. We always used to giggle about that – I don't know why!

I soon began to realise that cerebral palsy wasn't the only disability that people had. I met other children who had different disabilities, including haemophilia, cystic fibrosis, spina bifida. Sophie had spinal muscular atrophy. This is a genetic problem and affects physical strength because it damages the motor nerve cells in the spinal cord, causing progressive muscle weakness. This can eventually make it difficult for the person to walk, eat and even breathe, and in some cases, it will lead to an early death.

Physiotherapy was very much part of our day. I didn't really like doing it, but I had to get on with it because without this exercise it would be harder for me to walk because my legs can quickly become stiff. It was during these physio and exercise sessions that I discovered my love for swimming. Everyone used to call me a water baby. I sometimes used to go swimming every night because for me it was a way to escape for a bit. I loved being able to walk unaided, which I could do in the water; and for a moment, I would be free of the physical pain that accompanies cerebral palsy. The professionals told me that swimming was very good for me. However, I could never understand why I couldn't move my legs whilst swimming. My brain just was not sending the message to my legs to move. My arms completely compensated for the lack of movement from my legs, and they began to get very strong. There was one time when I was in the swimming pool and the fire alarm went off. I had to get out of the pool as quickly as possible (my arms really showed their strength at this point) and over to our house assembly point; and yes, I was still in my swimming costume. This is a moment that I won't forget!

At Lord Mayor Treloar College we had a hydrotherapy pool too. I went in this a couple of times to help me with my physio. The water was very hot which really relaxed my muscles. It was also very good for me after my operations to help me bend my legs. All I wanted to do really was swim, but it was clear that the hydrotherapy pool was not for that.

I used to spend lots of time in our games room. This is where I learnt how to play snooker and pool. We had both types of tables. Sophie taught me to play. It was such fun! People couldn't keep me away. I could hear people say, 'Where is Suz?'

The reply would be, 'Have you tried the games room? She will be in there!'

I had a friend called Simon Sedgwick. He had haemophilia. We often used to play snooker, but he was good, so I rarely won against him. I was often the champion against other people though!

Sophie and I used to pass the time by whizzing around in our chairs. Although not necessarily a hobby, you could argue it was a fun activity. I would be in mine, and I would hold onto the back of Sophie's electric chair. In the grounds of the lower school, we had an avenue, and Sophie and I used to go there sometimes. I would let go of her wheelchair and whizz to the bottom. It was so much fun. It wasn't as fun getting back up the hill though! Sophie always helped me.

The weekends at school dragged a bit at times. Some pupils went home, but for others, their family lived too far away, so they stayed at school. We spent Sunday mornings in church, but after that, we were free to do whatever we wanted. Depending on who was on duty, some staff would take us out and do cooking with us if that was what we wanted to do.

One Sunday Sophie and I were just talking, and I saw someone doing a wheelie. I told Sophie that I wanted to do one of those, so she taught me how to. To start with, I tipped my wheelchair back onto a bed, then gradually eased myself off the bed and started to balance on two wheels. It was scary at first, but I got the hang of it as I did it more and more. I thought this was great fun, although I'm not sure that the care staff felt the same as they looked at us with anxious expressions.

I was in Gaston House for a couple of years and then remained there one more year than I should have because there wasn't any space in the other houses. However, this didn't just apply to me; there were other pupils who didn't move out either. I didn't mind because I was with friends that I had known for a while and some who I had also known at my previous school; Brian Matthews, Tony Myres, Keith Smith and Julian Henley. I really liked Brian, but I didn't think that the feeling was reciprocated. He was shy and it didn't help that people used to tease us that we were boyfriend and girlfriend. Eventually, we did have a talk away from all his friends, and it was then that we shared a little kiss. It was my first, and I felt on cloud nine! We remained good friends throughout school, but there was no more romance.

On Saturday nights, we had toast in the evening. This was a real treat. We also were able to watch films, which meant staying the weekends at school wasn't too bad. There was a member of the care staff called Bobby. I really liked Bobby. I was always so pleased when she was on duty. We had such a laugh together. When I did get homesick, it was usually at the weekends. Bobby knew this so she always kept a close eye on me. She used to spoil me by making my favourite meal – spaghetti bolognese. Ali was another care staff who I got along with well. She used to help me make my bed. This was always a difficult job for me to do. My sister Rose took this role on when I wasn't at school. I used to tease Rosie by saying, 'Oh, but I sleep so much better when you make my bed'.

A couple of years passed, and it was time to move to a different house. There were spaces in Burnham House, so I moved there. Luckily, Sophie was moving there too; I was so relieved and happy that we would still be in the same house. Unfortunately, we weren't in the same dormitory, but we weren't too far away, and we made sure we were together during most of the day and evening. Burnham was very different to Gaston so it took some time to adjust; however, now we were older, we could stay up later, which was fun. We even had our own kitchen, which to me was a start to being more independent. We could make hot drinks, toast and other little snacks.

This is where Treloars really excelled. In hindsight, it was all about building us up to be independent, to preparing us for life in the outside world as a disabled person but preparing us in a very gradual and gentle way, with an understanding of our own individual limitations and our own individual pace. We were lucky that the staff guided us in this way. As a school, they had really thought through the best way to build this independence, and on reflection, it's not a straightforward process, and it's not a process that many other schools had to think about. It required thought, patience and attention. Treloars gave it just that, and I can honestly attribute a large percentage of my ability to be independent now to the time that I spent at Treloars.

Burnham also had a snooker table, so I was sorted! I played many games against the house master, Mr Scott. He was great fun, and his family were too. My confidence in my ability to play snooker was growing, and I began to win a few matches. We used to have snooker tournaments and once or twice, I got to the finals but unfortunately would then lose at the final stage. I was gutted! I knew I had to improve my game if I wanted to get the trophy, so I practised and practised.

My school report mentions my love for snooker but with the added advice of how I should also be encouraged in finding other hobbies and activities:

Suzie continues to enjoy playing snooker, but she should be encouraged to expand her interests. She should realise that it is not always possible to achieve everything but that nothing is achieved without trying it first. Suzie remains a pleasure to have in the house.

The words 'realise that it is not always possible to achieve everything' might help to explain my competitive streak *on the snooker table with Simon Sedgwick, my desire to win the tournaments and my determination to succeed when at first, I didn't.

On reflection, it was good that the staff at Treloars were encouraging me to take on different interests, because I did tend to fixate on one particular hobby, which might have meant I didn't get to experience the enjoyment of other activities, like swimming. But I always continued to have a love for snooker and still do now, to this day. I find it helps me to unwind.

At boarding school, you really got to know your friends so well and could spend all your time with them. They became like brothers and sisters. However, there were times when I would just want to have my own time, or to get away from it all or to have a change of environment. At a day school children go home in the evening and leave the school behind, but there really wasn't anywhere to go at boarding school to have time to yourself, and I sometimes found this hard.

After a year in Burnham House, I moved dormitories to the side wing. There was the option of having a double room here, so immediately Sophie and I picked a room to share. We had a TV in our bedroom, which was a real novelty for me. I also clearly remember having a yellow duvet cover that I really liked. I still love the colour yellow. Our bedroom was bright, and we had posters on the wall. I think some were of snooker players. I liked Steve Davis and Jimmy White in those days. I loved being on the side wing. It was a first step of freedom for me and the start of independence. We had to make our beds, which was an interesting experience. Duvet covers and I generally don't have a good understanding of one another.

A new term started and one of my good friends, Jenny, who had been a day pupil, became a weekly boarder. She had a single room just a few doors away from Sophie's and my room. Jenny had muscular dystrophy. There are different types of muscular dystrophy, but in most cases, it is an inherited condition with one or other of the parent being an unknown carrier of the gene. It is a muscle-weakening disease and is similar to the disability that Sophie had, but unlike spinal muscular atrophy, it is usually only apparent in males. Jenny was the first girl that I had met with this.

Jenny had a twin, which connected us instantly with a mutual understanding of the feelings associated with being a twin. Like Pips and me, her twin sister was able-bodied.

Jenny told me that she was part of a research project. From what I remember, the idea was that it was possible to use some bone marrow from Jenny's twin to help Jenny's condition by implanting it into Jenny's bone marrow. I'm sure it was much more complicated than this, but I remember that this was the gist of it. I noticed one day, as I saw Jenny walking down the corridor, how much more difficult it was for both Jenny and Sophie to walk than it was for me. It was noticeably hard for them, but they both kept going and going. I really hoped this research would help Jenny and work to prolong her life.

I remember Jenny having a Wispa chair made by Everest Jennings; and yes, I have the name right, it was not Cadburys! It was beige and I used to hold onto the back of it when I wanted a rest, as I did with Sophie's wheelchair. I admit it; I was very lazy! At least it meant that I could keep up with them both. Their wheelchairs were very fast, faster than I could walk.

Jenny, Sophie and I became firm friends. The school staff called us the 'terrible trio'. It was hard to see both Jenny's and Sophie's ability to walk deteriorate significantly as the months went by. It wasn't long from me seeing them able to walk to seeing them having to accept that they could no longer walk and therefore succumbing to a wheelchair. I was still mobile to an extent and rarely needed a wheelchair because I still had the use of my legs, albeit with the assistance of sticks. I used to wonder about how they felt when they realised that they could no longer walk. Did they know enough about their condition to realise that it would be such a progressive deterioration in this way? That it was life-limiting. It was a haunting thought.

The years at lower school seemed to go by so quickly. I really liked Burnham House, but I knew that I had to move on, and I was hoping for more independence with each move that I took. I found change hard, and I still do, but with family and friends around, and at school, particularly my friends, I knew it would be easier than doing it alone.

Evans House was where this move took me, and then our troublesome trio turned into a quality quartet! Sara joined our friendship group and we were all ready for our next adventure, in a new schoolhouse.

'Evans House, watch out. There's trouble about!'

It was slightly different in Evans House to how it was in Burnham House because we all had our own rooms. The girls were upstairs and the boys downstairs, but we had a communal kitchen and television room. I was in a corner room, and I remember it being nice and cosy.

The staff in Evans were great fun. I liked the housemaster, Ian Maddock. He had a wife, Sally, who was also nice, and they had two children, a daughter and a son. Ian liked rock climbing. Both he and Sally were very down-to-earth and full of fun. They made Evans House feel like one happy family, which made hard times at school easier. It was nice that the housemasters always integrated us with their families. Ian did this within Evans House, and Mr Scott did this within Burnham House. It gave us a real sense of belonging and comfort.

I have always had a love for music, and at the time, one of my favourite bands was Bros. Of course, they were twins; so again, I think I felt a natural affiliation. My friends used to call me a 'broset'. Please don't let this put you off reading the rest of my story! I'm not sure how much everyone else in Burnham House liked Bros, but I have a feeling that they soon got used to their music.

The requirement and desire to be independent set in once again; this seemed to increase the older I became and as the years went on. It was now up to me to get myself ready in time for breakfast, so I had to set my alarm rather than rely on the house staff to wake me. This was good for me and encouraged me to take on more responsibility for myself. I had to be ready by 8am, and most of the time I was ready in time. There was a rule in the lower school that we had to sit on set tables during the week, but at the weekend, we chose where we wanted to sit. I never really understood why this was, but I did understand that rules were rules.

After breakfast, we had to go back to our houses to get ready for lessons, and then it was off to assembly. Some students were already studying for A Levels, so they would get transport to Alton College. Sophie did A levels. She was very good at French and wanted to be a French interpreter. The rest of us would have lessons within the upper school campus.

At first, I was put in a class that I didn't really like. I think this was because I didn't do very well in tests. I remember having to write things down on a PAC card (Personal Achievement Card), and then I had to get it signed to show that I had done whatever it was. I remember having to write on this PAC that I had managed to tie my own shoelaces. Well, I guess we all must start somewhere!

During every lesson, I had to stand in a standing frame to help my legs straighten, ready for another operation. Standing in a frame for forty-five minutes was very painful. I used to call it the 'Torture Frame'. Thankfully it wasn't just me who had to go through this; there were others enduring the same. However, it soon became obvious that all the standing was an eventual blessing, building up my strength and balance. The drawback was that it was very hard to write anything down, so I just hoped that I wasn't ever asked to repeat back anything the teacher might have dictated to us because I never would have remembered without writing it down. Thankfully, the teachers didn't ask me to do this – they must have known!

On reflection, I really was quite naughty at school in the early years. I think it was because I was bored and I wasn't always challenged, but this also resulted in me not always trying my best. My father soon realised this and during one of the parents' evening he spoke with my teachers and the headteacher, about how I needed an aim, a focus, a goal. He was right, and when this was acknowledged I was put forward to study for GCSEs, which gave me that direction that I needed, and I started to concentrate more, listen in lessons and began to really enjoy learning. Not everyone had the ability to go through GCSEs, and I think the school thought this applied to me, but they hadn't even given me a chance. So, my father stepping in at this point and suggesting that I give GCSEs a go was entirely the right thing to do. It was late for me to start these exams in comparison to other teenagers my age, but better late than never, I thought. I didn't get top grades, but at least my attempt wasn't ungraded.

I used to think that during my time at boarding school, the teachers and carers could have given me more encouragement or self-belief that I could achieve all the things that an able-bodied person can. However, reading old school reports, I think they did. I started my time at school with little self-belief, and Treloars did a good job of building up my confidence.

Words from a report in 1987, following the Autumn term:

Suzie has been successful in many areas, and practical skills are considered to be good in science. She has reached a good standard in word processing. Apart from the two periods with a computer studies teacher, the class uses the word processor twice a week in English lessons. There is need to build up Suzie's self-esteem and self-worth. It is her fear of failure that affects her learning now. She is a delightful person with many personal qualities.

Three years later in 1990, extracts from my school report:

Suzie is a hard-working, well-motivated student with a lively, friendly personality. She has shown a maturity over academic disappointments and a determination to persevere and overcome the difficulties she experiences in certain areas of learning. There have already been improvements since last year due to her unfailing efforts, and hopefully, she will have some success with GCSE and Pitman examinations. Suzie is popular with her peers, gets on well with staff and is an asset in discussion groups.

My form tutor wrote those words, so it focused on my academic ability. In the same report, my housemaster also gave my parents and me some feedback about how I was getting on overall. This is what he wrote:

Clearly one of the most popular students with both staff and among her peer group. Suzie is a very confident young lady who, while working hard at life, can still greet the world with a warm smile.

Three years later, Treloars were telling my parents that I was growing in confidence and achieving academically. I think this is a great reflection of what Treloars gave to me, how the school supported me and helped me to develop both academically, and emotionally.

The first exam that I took was GCSE English. I was nervous, but I felt that I could do this. My parents had been so encouraging; telling me, 'Just do your best. We will be proud of you whatever the result.'

This is what I did; I did the best that I could, and I passed! The grade I got wasn't a high grade by 'university' standards, but at least it was graded. This made me feel as proud as punch, as I told Sophie later. She was so proud of me. I think even the teachers saw a change in my attitude towards working, which was what I always wanted. I later took another GCSE – Modular Science. I passed this too. I was beginning to flourish and have genuine confidence in my academic ability.

The time had come for me to start thinking about what I wanted to do once I left school. I had always wanted to work in an office, so I decided to do a CPVE (Creative Pre-Vocational Education course) in Business Studies.

Most of my lessons took place in a building called the Trail Centre. This was a very light, open-planned, stylish building, located in the school grounds. Staff on the reception desk greeted you as you came in. I loved going over to the Trail Centre. I could push myself across there from the main school and so it felt as if I had escaped from school. It was less like a boarding school and more like an office environment, which I really liked. There were different departments within the building, a typing area, a computing section, a CDT (Craft Design and Technology) place, a music room and a dark room. I loved photography so I was often in the dark room.

We were encouraged to cover all subjects as part of the course, and then at the end, we could choose what we enjoyed the most. It was good to get experience in all these different areas because it left our options open.

I soon crossed CDT off my list of subjects that I wanted to

continue. I just didn't get on well with it. I loved music and computing, so these two stayed at the top of my list. I had never been hugely academic, but I could sense that the teachers noticed how much I wanted to achieve in this course and were supportive.

We also had to do lessons on a Saturday morning. This meant that if we were planning to go home for a weekend we did not leave until 12pm, except for a 'leave weekend' when we were allowed to go home on Fridays. I stayed at school most weekends because it didn't seem worth going home for just one night; no sooner had you got home, it felt as if it was time to come back again!

However, I did try to go home on leave weekends if I could, when I could spend two nights away from school. For the three years that my parents were living in Zimbabwe, I would go to my maternal grandparents' house for the weekend. These were the same grandparents who used to take us to the airport for our flight out to Zimbabwe and pick us up when we returned. They lived in a sweet little farmhouse in Wiltshire, and we always had such a lovely time. I very much enjoyed going to stay there. My sisters were at a different boarding school to me, so we tried to coordinate the weekends so we could all be at my grandparents' house together, but this often depended on when they were able to have a weekend away from school. The weekends used to go far too quickly.

We called my grandmother Bamma. The name Bamma emerged because Jenny, when she was young and learning to talk, couldn't say the word Grandma and in her attempts, said Bamma. Bamma was an excellent cook, and we spent lots of time in the kitchen, chatting and eating the delicious food that seemed to be in endless supply from the Aga: sausages, croissants, fresh bread. It was a cosy room. The walls in the kitchen had some impressive drawings on them painted by my mother. This added to the authenticity of the room and the house itself. Being in this family environment was just what we all needed when we came home from a boarding school that was more clinical and much less homely. I remember doing many jigsaws with Bamma. They were often quite large jigsaws, which would spread right across the kitchen table. It was a lovely way to spend time relaxing with her and chatting. And if we weren't assembling jigsaws, we were probably playing scrabble. Grandpa would often be sitting in his chair, which was in the corner of the kitchen. Every now and again he would nod off to sleep, but when we called his name, he was instantly awake, claiming to be just 'shutting his eyes'. We would all giggle. If we weren't in the kitchen, we were in a little television room, adjacent to the kitchen, having some tea and watching various television programmes. Bamma and Grandpa had two cats and a dog. I particularly loved one of the cats, Polly, who used to come and sit on my lap and purr quietly.

My grandparents were very active in the village community, and my sisters and I also liked to get involved. We would help with the summer fetes, various village functions. Jenny used to sing in the church choir, and my grandfather was one of the church wardens. It was a lovely and lively village and a happy place to be.

I have such fond memories of my time at the farmhouse. We were so lucky to have this second home whilst my parents were away and such loving grandparents to welcome us in, always with open arms. Bamma and Grandpa were truly our lifeline at this time, both for my sisters and me, and for my parents, who could relax knowing that we were being well looked after, in a warm and loving family home, by people who genuinely cared for us.

I hated it when either the weekend or a half-term ended and I had to go back to school. Grandpa used to take me back on a Sunday night, but very occasionally, he would drive me back early on a Monday morning, which meant I could spend that extra night away from school.

I always settled back into school quickly though, once I saw my friends and got back into the school routine. One lesson I really enjoyed was the music lessons. A group from our school entered a music competition. They had composed a song called 'Don't Chase the Dragon', which won them the competition and gave the school some prize money, which they put towards the cost of building a recording studio. My group wrote a couple of songs just for fun; but we still got them recorded and put onto a tape (we didn't have CDs in those days!), which was exciting and meant a lot to us. I had always wanted to play the drums but unfortunately, my legs just wouldn't coordinate. The involuntary spasms meant that I could never stay on beat.

Other lessons that we did included cooking; this was an experience and a half! Unfortunately, my attempts at being a Jamie Oliver invariably resulted in some sort of burning. I even managed to set the fire alarm off at one point. This made me quite unpopular. The teacher was a little scary. She used to shout and pronounce the end of her words so forcefully that it would make me jump (but at least I knew my reflexes were working!) Then she would ask me what I was up to; I used to think, 'I haven't moved a muscle, I'm just trying to listen.' I safely concluded that I would never get my own cooking show! On one occasion, I even managed to burn soup. Needless to add, my cooking skills haven't really improved much.

In and amongst our lessons at Lord Mayor Treloar College, I have been fortunate enough to meet an actor or two. I met the actor Robert Powell. He opened a room in the Trail Centre, named after him. I also met the radio presenter Simon Mayo. He was a laugh! Having listened to him so much on the radio, it was so nice to meet him in person.

Then there was the arrival of a member of the royal family to our school. It was all very exciting. On the morning of the visit, the cleaners were tirelessly scrubbing the floors. I had never seen them look so clean!

Lady Diana flew in by helicopter. Thankfully, it was a lovely day; the sun was shining and we were all sitting comfortably with a good view. I was sitting in my wheelchair in the front row. I must admit to being nervous. I just hoped that my words would come out if she spoke to me, which she did. She shook my hand and asked, 'How are you?'

I replied, 'I am very well, thank you,' adding, 'It is so nice to meet you!'

As I could have predicted, my legs did their usual involuntary spasm and promptly kicked Lady Diana's leg. I apologised profusely, explaining that they had a mind of their own. She totally understood and did not seem to think much of it, but it was still so embarrassing! I couldn't disguise my stutter either (which I will write more about later in this book). Once again, I wished that I did not have these symptoms of cerebral palsy, just for this one occasion. This magical time of meeting and speaking briefly with Lady Diana will stay with me for the rest of my life. I felt so privileged to be part of the special day. It's not every day you meet a member of the royal family.

At another time the Prince of Wales visited Lord Mayor Treloar College although I didn't get a chance to speak with him, which was a shame.

I then met Princess Anne, on another occasion, at the local riding school that I went to on a Tuesday afternoon. We put a little show on for her on our horses, and guess who the leader was? Me! Thankfully, I remembered all the routines that we had practised; people were relying on me to show them the steps. It could have gone horribly wrong if I had forgotten. I was so glad I didn't let anyone down. Princess Anne loved the show and came to chat with all of us afterwards, whilst we were still on our horses. My horse behaved well whilst she spoke to us, which was a blessing; otherwise, I could have had another embarrassing royal moment! Apparently, my grandfather, who had come to this special event, met Princess Anne behind the horse box, and they had quite a chat!

I include all the occasions that I have been lucky enough to meet famous people because I appreciate every opportunity that I got.

Re-reading my reports in later years, I was pleased to come across the following words from the headmaster, in the Autumn of 1990. Again, another reflection of how well I was developing, and how the school were helping me along.

> *With the effort and determination that Suzie has continued to put into her work she really deserves to have some examination success. She shows great perseverance in coping with her difficulties and deserves praise for this. She has matured into a really super young lady with a warm and friendly manner. She is at ease with the many visitors who come to the college and can be relied upon to show them around effectively. She has been very supportive in her house and helpful to her new housemaster, and her friends value her considerate and kind nature.*

As I have mentioned, we were encouraged to be as independent as possible at school: preparing us for the outside world. We had the opportunity to live in a flat where we could trial our independence. In order to determine if we were ready to live on our own, we had to achieve two levels of independence. The first level was to demonstrate that we could plan our meals; go to the supermarket, use money we had been given to buy the ingredients, and then come home to cook it (thank goodness for those cooking lessons; although I steered clear of making soup!). We had supervision through all of this, which also helped to determine if we really were ready to be this independent. I very much enjoyed the whole experience, particularly buying and preparing my own meal; it beat having to sit and eat with the rest of the students in the school!

Once we had passed this level, we moved to the next level, which was to not only buy and prepare our own meals, but also to stay overnight in the flat, make sure it was always clean, and then organise ourselves to be ready for school on time. I did find it much harder to manage all of this; however, once I found a routine it became easier. I knew that this is what I would have to do if I wanted to live on my own or with other people, independently. I would need to be organised, and I hoped I would have a job, so putting this into practice in a safe environment helped me to appreciate what I needed to be able to do. It also made me thankful for what my parents do; how much they had to plan and organise to look after my sisters and me. I was so pleased with myself that I achieved independent living at school and that this paved a way for me later in my life.

I think there were times when the staff and teachers just didn't want to raise hopes, or my expectations, so possibly veered on the side of caution when talking to us all about what life would be like once we left school, which I can very much understand. For me, it was also my family, my parents, who really urged me to have a go at all those things that I thought I wouldn't be able to achieve.

Every person with a disability is individual, despite having the same disability as someone else. It is very difficult to predict what each person might or might not be able to achieve; therefore it's important to give each individual person the opportunity to have a go. Treloars understood this and managed us all individually, always being mindful and realistic of our ability.

The next big challenge of independence was learning to drive. It was fortunate that Lord Mayor Treloar College had a driving instructor on site. His name was John Smith. I remember going for my first driving assessment. I had to see if I would be able to use my feet. Unfortunately, the assessment concluded that I couldn't as my reactions were too slow – but don't worry, the engine was turned off, so we didn't end up half a mile down the road in seconds! I soon learnt that a car could be adapted with hand controls, so I learnt to drive using push and pull control, with a single steering wheel spanner. These are like what tractors have. There was a lever on the right side of the steering wheel, which I pushed up to go faster and pushed down to break. Attached to this I had a flick switch indicator. I had to have the accelerator pedal removed otherwise my legs might have gone under it and then got jammed (which would have sent me and the car and any unsuspecting passengers off in all sorts of directions!). I found out later that I could get an additional pedal if someone else wanted to, or needed to, drive the car but wanted to use the foot adaptions, rather than the hand controls. Most of my family got used to driving the way that I did with the hand controls, so there wasn't much need for the pedals, but it was good to know that they could be fitted if required.

By the end of my time at Treloars, I was not ready to take a test, but I was confident enough and fit for the road, so I continued with driving lessons after I left school and was living at home.

My independence had increased massively thanks to Treloars, and my school days were now ending. It was time to say goodbye; not only to a boarding school that I had been part of for so many years, which had become my second home, but also goodbye to my friends, some of who I would never see again. For two of my very best friends, this goodbye came far too early, and it wasn't a goodbye that any of us wanted to say. Their disability finally stole their lives and they died before their time.

Before I write about my final goodbyes to my friends who were like sisters to me, I have included a poem written about 'school days'.

School Days

School days were hard for me
Boarding it just had to be
I got used to it eventually
And it all fell into place naturally
Time tables were here and there
It felt like there was no time to spare
Teachers were everywhere.

Physio was twice a week
This taught me how to get on my feet
By the end I began to feel at my peak
Stretches here and there
Torture is not fair
But it was for my own good
So it ended to be "all good in the hood"

I had one special friend
Which I'm sure at times I drove around the bend
We raced each other in our chairs
It was like being at one big fair
Spinning around everywhere
It was fun that we both shared
Our tyres would lose grip
But it did make us feel fit
Just for a little bit.

I loved sports days
They were held on Bank Holidays
Which happened to be in the month of May
I swam until my heart was content
Which gave me lots of confidence
To go fast it was a blast.

There were good times, bad times
And very tough times too
But this taught me that I had to see school through
And face reality in the hope that I'm a stronger person too.
I couldn't wait to get out
To check what life was about
Challenges I face which I do with grace
And at my own pace
So please continue to watch this big space.

Chapter 6

Last of the school days

My last two years at Lord Mayor Treloar College were a mixture of emotions and a mixture of goodbyes. I had blossomed in my education, achieving more than I thought was possible. I was given goals to work towards, GCSEs and courses to complete, and I thrived on these challenges. I was going to say goodbye to a school I had been part of for so long, a place that had supported, and nurtured me, that had provided an education for me, and where I had gained invaluable independence. I knew I needed to take all these skills and hit the big wide world head-on. However, the darker side of the goodbyes was facing up to the fact that my two best friends wouldn't live beyond their teenage years, due to their disabilities. I was distraught. I couldn't and didn't want to believe that this could happen to people so young. I had no choice, I had to say goodbye to them both; it was out of anyone's control.

When Sophie died, I felt numb. It was horrible. I remember being told the devastating news when I was in Modular Science; I was doing an experiment at the time. There was a knock on the door. I instantly knew something was wrong. I could tell by my housemaster's expression on his face. He asked me to go outside and told me that Sophie had passed away.

I screamed, 'No, no, this can't be true.'

It had only been about an hour before that one of the house staff had said that Sophie was due to come back to school. How did they get this so wrong? She had been in hospital with a chest infection, which was the second time in the last few weeks.

I remember visiting Sophie in sickbay. She was in room 007. I had also stayed in this same room a couple of months earlier. Her last ever words to me were 'I was in the same room as you in the hospital.'

I went back to my room and played some music. I think it was Tracy Chapman. To me, it just seemed like a dream. It didn't seem true. I felt so alone and just didn't know what to do. Sophie was my rock; she had helped me so much over the years. I remembered the times that I had a very bad stutter and lots of people used to think it was funny to tease me and stutter back at me, making fun of me. It was horrible and made me not want to speak. Sophie always used to help me, stand by me, and say, 'Don't worry, Suz. They're the ones with the problem, not you.'

There were other times when Sophie was such a support when I had just had another operation on my legs to help straighten them. The operation had loosened and lengthened my hamstrings. I remember Sophie used to push me to do my exercises. I used to walk in the corridors with her by my side in her electric wheelchair, and she would say, 'Come on, Suz. You can do it!'

And I did. I was so pleased to be doing this for her and for me. She told me she was as proud as punch for me. Without Sophie's support, I doubt I would have got as far as I did with my walking.

Life was so hard after Sophie had died, but I had to try and get used to it, and I did try. Sophie was not the only student in the school to die before their time. There were others too. You always knew when it had happened because the staff would ask us to go back to our houses and then they would tell us. When Sophie died, I think the staff knew that they needed to speak to me alone, to give me time to process it before they made an announcement to all the other pupils in the school. This must have been why they took me out of Modular Science. They knew how close we were.

Three months after Sophie had passed away my other friend Jenny, who was part of our foursome friendship group, went into hospital because she had a chest infection. I went to see her and as we were saying goodbye, she said to me, 'Don't break anything, Suz!'

I said, 'I will try not to, Jenny!'

She knew that I was going on a skiing holiday with the school to Switzerland to a place called Gstaad.

A few days later, after I had just had breakfast, the staff told me that Jenny had passed away. I couldn't believe it. From our foursome friendship group, it was now just Sara and me. I didn't feel like going on the skiing holiday at all. I felt devastated, again. I knew Jenny would have wanted me to carry on, and go on the skiing holiday, so I did, but with a heavy heart.

The research project that Jenny had been part of (where they were taking bone marrow from Jenny's twin to inject back into Jenny in the hope of helping Jenny's condition) to slow the muscular dystrophy down, was not completed. We will never know if this could have helped Jenny because she lost her life too soon. There was a plan to televise the research project, so the production team came to our school and interviewed some of Jenny's close friends, which included me. To my intense frustration, I had hoped to record this television programme, but I ended up getting the time right but the channel wrong! I was so annoyed.

I missed her funeral because I was still in Switzerland. I felt like I never said a proper goodbye. I always try to remember the good times we had, but it is hard. RIP to all my friends. You were all very special to me.

Skiing was great fun. I knew Jenny would have wanted me to enjoy myself, so I really did try, despite feeling devastated that I would never see her again.

This was the second skiing holiday that I had been on, but I was still no expert. When the teachers at school had first mentioned skiing, I hadn't realised that it was even an option for me. My first thought was that I would probably spend more time *in* the snow than *on* it! However, this is probably true for anyone learning such a balancing act.

I was given a pair of skis to try first, and I had the two poles to hold either side of the skis to help with balance; a similar set-up to what any able-bodied person would be given. The only difference was that I was attached to the instructor using a rope, which they fastened around my waist. The instructor would slowly start to ski down the slope, pulling me forward behind them, whilst I concentrated on keeping my balance.

It was a wonderful feeling, and for some prolonged moments, I felt as if I was just like anyone else learning to ski. However, concentration was essential at this point, as with the slightest lapse, my face met with the snow, which ended up being more often than I would have liked.

So, the instructors suggested a different technique. This involved a type of toboggan. It was really a skiing wheelchair, but I preferred to think of it as a toboggan. I would sit in a chair that had skis on the bottom and again, I had two poles to give me the ability to get moving and control my direction, and then I was off! On one occasion though, I gathered up a little too much speed and saw myself heading to the edge of the slope, beyond which I anticipated a huge drop. The only way to stop was to topple over and land in the snow on my side, which I did, just in time, as I saw the edge of the slope approaching fast. This experience did inject an element of caution in me for future attempts, and I was more careful.

Skiing really was a wonderful opportunity for me, and for the time I was in Gstaad it did allow me to put aside my grief of losing Jenny, although she was never far from my thoughts.

Treloars had really given all the pupils at the school so many opportunities to travel, explore and do these adventurous, sporting activities so we could enjoy and partake in the same experiences as any able-bodied person. Only a year before, the school had organised for us to go on an outbound course in the Lake District. As the name suggests, we didn't do much sitting around and were instead out and about every day trying a new outdoor sport. On one very memorable occasion, we climbed the 'Catbells Mountain'. I can't quite remember how we climbed the mountain; I think it was a combination of some walking and some pushing myself in a wheelchair. I just remember it gave me the most enormous buzz! It helped that I had a rather nice chap who stood beside me to lend me a hand should I have needed it.

But my time at the school was coming to an end. One of my last reports was this:

> *This year has been marked by Suzie's sheer determination to succeed in her course. She is very sensible and well-motivated and will ask for help when she has a problem. I do hope that she is successful in the examinations which she has taken recently. In her house, she has been most supportive, both to her friends and members of staff. We are so sorry that she had to cope with so much sadness. She has displayed considerable fortitude, and I do hope that next year will be kinder to her. The staff accompanying the skiing trip were most impressed by the determination and skill which she showed, and I understand that there is great promise for the future. Well done, Suzie.*

It was very touching reading this in my adult years. Treloars understood how I must have felt when two of my best friends died, and they commented on my determination, both in my studies and in my sport. It meant a lot to have this recognition, and it reminded me of all that the school had done for me to help me be the person that I am today.

When I returned from skiing, I knew that the time was approaching for me to leave Lord Mayor Treloar College. I had been there for ten years. I knew I was ready to move on with the next chapter in my life, but what was I going to do? One of the staff at the school suggested that I stay in a residential home; I immediately said, 'No!'

I was adamant that I wanted to go to my local college. My careers adviser asked me quite blatantly if I would be able to cope.

'Yes,' I said, with all the conviction that I felt. My parents were fully behind me on my decision to do this. I wanted to do something in the Business Administration area because it still was my dream to work in an office.

I first had to pass the course I was currently doing, the CPVE in Business Administration. I wouldn't know if I had passed it until July. I had everything crossed!

As part of the Business Administration course, we had to do two weeks work experience. I had the opportunity to work at the police headquarters in Winchester. Every morning I would travel there. The school provided transport for me. I did administrative tasks. It was all good practice for me, giving me a taste of what life was going to be like after Lord Mayor Treloar. I loved every minute of it. My colleagues were so nice. I certainly felt part of the team. My manager assessed me on everything I did, and how well I did it, or not! I found some tasks difficult, but it was obvious that I wanted to achieve all that I could. I had my sights set high! At the end of the two weeks work experience, my manager sent a report back to my tutor at the college.

My hard work paid off and the report on me at the end was

good. They even said that if I had lived nearer there would have been a chance of employment at the headquarters. My work experience report did count to my final mark for my CPVE in Business Administration, so I was on cloud nine that it was good.

In my final report, in the summer of 1991, my form tutor wrote this:

> *Although Suzie has continued to find some aspects of her course difficult to cope with, she has remained a cheerful, hard-working student determined to do her best. In all areas, academic, sport and social, she is a well-liked popular student whose lively personality makes her an asset to any group. Suzie should be awarded her certificate of pre-vocational education before she leaves, and I hope she will have success in her AEB and Pitman examinations and also GCSE. Next year she will be attending a college in her local area to continue her studies, and if her recent work experience in Winchester is anything to go by, I am sure she will have no problem meeting new friends and fitting in well. Good luck, Suzie.*

I had one final holiday to enjoy with the school. Again, I'm so grateful to Treloars for giving me this opportunity. A group of us went to Holland. It was awesome. I went on a catamaran, which I absolutely loved. I couldn't sit up though because of the speed the catamaran was going so I just lay on my front whilst watching the waves coming over the sides. I was screaming with excitement. I also did some canoeing. I loved this too, until I capsized, and my legs wouldn't bend; that was a bit frightening, but luckily there was always a member of staff close at hand. It was a great holiday.

When I returned from Holland, I heard that I had been accepted at the local college. So, all my hard work paid off. Now all I had to do was keep this determination and motivation going.

The time came when I had to say goodbye to Treloars and face the outside world. I can't deny that I was nervous, but I was very excited too. It was up to me now. I was solely responsible for setting my alarm, getting ready in time for appointments. There was no room for excuses! At boarding school, I always had someone to help, to fall back on, to make sure I wasn't going to be late. It was going to be good practice for me to do this for myself, and I knew in my heart that I was ready.

I had some good times at the Lord Mayor Treloar College, but there were some sad times too, particularly when my friends passed away and I said those final, emotional goodbyes. However, it made me realize how lucky I was. I did get frustrated that I couldn't walk like everyone else, but at least I could walk. My view is that there are always people worse off, and this kept me going and made me appreciate what I did have in life. I had accepted that I couldn't change the way I was, so I had to just get on with it, and that's just what I did!

So let the hard work of earning money now begin!

However, not before including a poem that I wrote for my two friends who left this world too early, who both lived a life with such fulfilment and good spirit, but whose lives were tragically taken away from them when their disability overcame their ability to survive.

They were both 'precious hearts'.

Precious Hearts

Precious hearts are hard to find
But when you do, your heart feels new
And the beat will be very close to you
So cherish this forever and it will comfort you
And it will always be there with you.

We never forget loved ones and think of them each day
I look to the sky and want to say "Hi"
The stars are bright which makes me feel alright
We talk all night which makes me feel bright.

The clouds move slow hey ho hey ho
Precious hearts in heaven get into a nice flow
Altogether they race and think this is ace
But must slow down to a good pace
So that they can all embrace in a very good place
The love heaven shares to all the precious hearts in this part
Is filled with a sparkle, which is remarkable
So remember the above line and everything will be fine.

Our love is always there for you
And it will be very fair
For the warmth that comes from the heart
It will fill a very big part that will never come apart
Remember this and it will be bliss
We will meet one day and all say hooray
And pray for a very good day.

Chapter 7

Working

It was a big step, leaving Lord Mayor Treloar College. My time there had equipped me well for life in the real world and I was ready to give it all a go. Talking with my parents, we agreed on three main aims for me: to pass my driving test, to find a job, and to live independently, in that order. All were achievable, but it would take time and some hard work, but with the support of my family and friends, I knew that I could do this.

I quickly resumed driving lessons to get myself ready for the road. There was a mobility scheme, which meant that I could have my own car that was adapted to suit my needs, like the one that I had driven at Treloars during my lessons with John Smith. Having my own car through the mobility scheme allowed me to practice with my father patiently sitting in the passenger seat. This combined with lessons meant that I was eventually ready for my test.

The conditions of a driving test for me were the same as for an able-bodied person except that the examiners gave me more time to do the test. It took a few tries, but I got there in the end and passed the third time. I finally got a licence for the road on November 26th, 1992.

Having achieved this first aim, learning to drive, I continued to focus on furthering my education, which I had been doing in parallel with learning to drive. I had completed an RSA diploma course at our local college in Salisbury, which had recently merged with the art college where my mother had studied. It was nice knowing that I was within an establishment and building that my mother had been part of years before. This course taught me a variety of computerised administrative skills, such as word processing, which would be useful for me if I wanted to pursue a career in the secretarial area, which I did.

I won't deny the element of shock from leaving the close community of Treloars to attending a college where I was the only disabled person in the year. It was a major crossover into 'real life', and I realised that being at school had offered some protection on what life was really going to be like.

I quickly learnt that in the real world I had to plan my own time and make sure I wasn't late for lessons. Getting from one place to another took much more planning for me than it would for an able-bodied person. In the early stages, before I could drive, I had to plan my lift and be on time to be picked up and dropped off (there were no mobile phones!). I hadn't really had to worry about this or think much about this at school, because it was all in one place and there were so many facilities in the school which were adapted for wheelchairs and students with disability. It was a challenge fitting into an environment where there aren't always the allowances for someone who is disabled and where my daily struggles were somewhat more than other people's. But I did it!

The teachers and staff at the college were so supportive. They gave me the opportunity to have extra lessons in my free periods when the other students went to town. My proudest moment at the college was achieving this RSA diploma. A few of the other students and I even got to meet the RSA examiner. This gave me a feeling of acceptance, that people were accepting me as Suz and not as the girl with the disability. Before going to the college, I had constantly been around disabled people during my school years. I was initially apprehensive when starting at the college because I wondered how people would react to me having a disability, but my group were fantastic with me. I still keep in touch through social media with a girl from the group.

During this course, which I completed in July 1992, I did some work experience in the personnel department. I later discovered that a section called Student Services was going to be opened within the collage, and I couldn't believe my luck when the personnel officer asked if I would be interested in a job within this department. I was over the moon that they had asked me, and I immediately replied with, 'Yes, I really would. Thank you.'

He said that he had been impressed with me during the work experience that I had done previously as part of the RSA diploma course. The next step was to apply for the job and hope that they selected me. I knew most of the staff from doing the work experience; I had liked them all, and I hoped that they had like me, so I was quietly confident. I found out only weeks later that I had been successful, so I started full-time employment in September 1992, as a clerical assistant. Both my parents and I were so pleased that I had managed to find work. What a relief, and so quickly.

So many thoughts began to buzz around in my head; questions such as, would I be fast enough at my job? What if I needed to carry things but couldn't? How would people treat me? I felt that having a disability would inevitably have its limitations, and even though I had tried to be as independent as possible, I knew that there were probably going to be some things that I just couldn't do.

A friend told me that there was a charitable organisation called the Shaw Trust. I decided to look further into what they did, and I was amazed when I discovered exactly what they did do. Their main goal was to help disabled and disadvantaged people into employment and independent living whilst providing ongoing support. This was exactly the support that I needed. I knew it was hard for anyone to find employment, even without the added disadvantage of a disability, so now that I had a job, I was glad to know that the Shaw Trust could support me and help me find some suitable accommodation so that I could move out of home and live independently.

Things were looking bright for me. A meeting was set up for me to meet a development officer from the Shaw Trust. I was introduced to a nice and friendly guy. We talked through the job that Student Services were offering me and discussed what aspects of it I might find difficult. As a clerical assistant, I would mainly be sitting behind a desk answering the phone, booking appointments and sending out prospectuses. Most of the job I was sure I could do, but I knew I would find filing and lifting difficult due to my issues regarding balance and feeling unstable without holding onto my sticks.

My development officer told me about a scheme called Access to Work. This scheme helps with equipment in the workplace for people with disabilities. It provides equipment such as scooters, trolleys, chairs (both electric and manual) and stationary. With my limited mobility, I knew that this offer of physical support would make it so much easier for me to get around. The first piece of equipment that I got was a chair. It was fantastic. I could move the back of the chair up and down to suit my needs. It was so comfortable. I did have to be careful that I didn't relax too much and fall asleep on the job! This obviously never happened.

I remember my first day as a working person. I was so proud that I had found employment. It helped so much that the people who I was working with knew me, and so they knew my limitations due to the cerebral palsy. It was a relief that I didn't have to explain why I couldn't carry some items or walk up and down the stairs.

I worked alongside two other women in Student Services who were also administration officers. We were all responsible for keeping the department running smoothly and offering help to students when they needed it. Other staff in the team included the Student Services manager, a counsellor, a finance officer and a careers adviser. The careers adviser would come into the office twice a week and would be available to the students if they had questions or uncertainties about their future career.

An understanding of how to use the computers in the office was essential, so I was pleased that I had completed the RSA course. There was a computer programme called Kudos that I thought was particularly clever. It worked by presenting the user with questions about what they liked to do and then matching these interests to a potential career. It was fun but it didn't always get it right. One day I decided to have a go. I answered all the questions it was asking me, about what I liked doing and what my strengths were, and it suggested to me that I might like to pursue a career as a carpet fitter! I had to laugh. It certainly didn't have that right, considering I can barely kneel. Regardless of this miss-match, Kudos did seem to work well for most of the students, matching their interests to the right employment. I can only put it down to it having a bad day when I used it!

We kept prospectuses of other universities and colleges in our department. The students used to come in and spend hours looking at them as well as our own prospectuses. It was a full-time job in itself to make sure all the prospectuses were up to date, but it was all good fun and I found it interesting. I hadn't realised that there were so many opportunities to become educated in so many different areas.

I settled into my role quickly. The students were always very kind and patient with me, and I built up quite a good rapport with them. When they walked past Student Services, I would usually get a wave from a few of them!

One day, to my complete surprise, a journalist from the local paper appeared outside the college and asked to speak with me. I was totally stuck for words (which doesn't happen very often!). What did they want? I found out that they wanted to write an article on me, a disabled person who had found employment with the help of the Shaw Trust. The article would be a way to share with the local community that there is help available for people with disabilities to find employment. It was suddenly very exciting that I was the first disabled employee to have a job at the college, and now I was going to be in the local paper. Wow! It can be hard enough to find employment if you are able-bodied so, if you have a disability, it is even harder, and some employers don't even give us the chance. I was very lucky.

The Shaw Trust also offered holidays for disabled people, of which I took full advantage several times, and I had a great time on the various holidays that I went on. It was all organised for us; the trust selected the accommodation with our disabilities in mind, and they planned various activities for disabled people to keep us busy from the moment we arrived. I met some lovely people on these holidays, and we always had good fun, even if at times, we partied a little too hard! It was so refreshing to be doing what other abled-bodied people could do so easily, but also nice to be around other people who shared the same frustrations as me but who could let it all go when they were on holiday.

In and amongst the holidays I continued to love my job, but at times, it was challenging. As a department, we received any new literature about the various courses. This could be about the course itself or about the finance of a course. It was important that Student Services had the most recent information on all courses at any time, which often made my job very busy. I relied on the tutors to provide me with this information so I could check the prospectus, but during holiday time, they were often not around, and yes, even though it was a college, I didn't get the same time off as the students! However, it did mean that whilst I worked during the college holiday time, the office was less busy so I could catch up and not worry about attending to other tasks immediately as was often the case when there were students coming into the office with various requests.

I answered the phone regularly but there is one occasion that will always stick in my mind. A caller wanted a prospectus of our college. As I was writing his details, he said, 'You're very slow at writing, aren't you?'

I said, 'Yes. but I want to get your address right.'

He was quiet after that. He obviously didn't know that I had a disability because he couldn't see me! What he didn't know and what he couldn't see, was that I found it hard writing whilst holding a phone at the same time. I did try a phone headset, but this didn't help much because the office was very noisy, and the headset did even less to keep this external noise out. I would often ask the caller to spell out or repeat what they were saying. This gave me a bit more time to make sure I had written all the information down correctly.

For other tasks that I found difficult due to my disability, such as filing or placing books back onto a shelf, for example, my colleagues were so good to me and always offered to help. In return, I would do other jobs for them, like shredding, which no one really liked to do. I don't know what it is about shredding, but I find it relaxing. We worked well as a team.

The saying is 'A change is as good as a rest'. Well, there was no doubt things were changing in Student Services with more courses on the horizon. After a few years, a new Student Services manager also joined us. She had previously worked for the careers service, so she had lots of knowledge on courses that were available and how to fill in UCAS/PCAS forms, which are the forms used when students want to go onto higher education, for courses such as a Higher National Diploma. This was useful as I wasn't that familiar with the UCAS and PCAS forms. Overall, Student Services was buzzing, buzzing, all day! Sometimes it was hard to escape for a break, but we all made sure that we did catch some time out; otherwise, we knew our work would suffer. My colleagues and I came up with a rota system for lunches. It worked very well.

I still found it hard to move around the office due to the number of people that were nearby. It wasn't just the staff, but also there was usually a steady flow of students coming in and out of the office, picking up prospectuses or asking questions. The students were all so kind and often offered to help me if they could see that I was struggling, but independence was everything to me, so I only accepted their offer of help if I really needed it! They all began to realise that.

Walking with my sticks gave me some form of independence, allowing me to move about and walk on my own. Having passed my driving test and now with a car, I was driving myself into work. One day, I arrived at work, following the usual routine of getting ready, getting in the car and driving. After I had parked, and just as I was opening the car door, I realised with a sense of absolute disbelief, that my sticks were not in the car with me but were instead still on the ground, in the driveway, at home. I had totally forgotten to pick them up and put them in the car. My heart totally sank. I couldn't believe it! My sticks were my lifeline. Mobile phones didn't exist in those days, so I couldn't make a phone call to home, or to anyone, from the car. I simply had to wait until someone walked past so that I could ask for help. Eventually, I spotted someone who readily came over and helped me to walk into the office; me clutching their arm to keep me steady, so that I could make the phone call home. It was at that moment, and I have lived through other similar moments, that I really did wish that my legs worked properly. As soon as my mother got the message, she immediately got in the car and drove across the town to give me back my sticks. It was certainly a learning experience, and I never made that mistake again! I can look back and laugh about it now, but it wasn't amusing at the time.

I saw my development officer from the Shaw Trust on a monthly basis and more often if I needed to. During one of these meetings, she suggested that I try using an electric scooter. She told me I could purchase one through the Access to Work scheme. Initially, I thought the office would never be big enough, especially when we had an influx of students, which happened quite regularly. However, I had to think logically. It would be easier for me, I would get less tired and maybe I would be quicker. Tasks like answering the phone, or writing down information would be easier, because I would already be sitting down and therefore wouldn't need to walk to a desk, slowly sit down before answering the phone, for example. It was a slow process for me, making my way back to a desk and then sitting down; I had to be careful not to lose my balance and fall. I needed the other staff in the office to agree, as I didn't want to aggravate any of them, so after some consultation with them, I decided to try an electric scooter. However, my whizzing around the office was short-lived. At times, it was impossible to move about without nearly running people over. I eventually decided to give the scooter a miss and reclaim my sticks, which had always served me well.

Just over a year of starting work at the college, my parents found me a warden-assisted ground floor flat. This was my next step to achieving independence. It was really exciting. My parents took me to see the flat, and I loved it! It had other young people living in other flats within the building, and it seemed to be exactly the right place for me. The kitchen and bathroom were adapted to meet the needs of a person in a wheelchair. Although I didn't spend much time at all in a wheelchair, it did mean that I could easily navigate my way around my kitchen sitting down, which made it much easier to cook, clean and tidy up. In the bathroom there was a seat in the shower area, again, making it easier for me to enjoy a shower. The day came when I moved in. I was so proud. I had done it. I had set out with three aims, to drive, to have a job, and to live independently. With the help and support from my family, I had achieved all three. It was a dream come true.

Although I had practised living independently at school, this was different, and this was going to be permanent. I lived close to my parents, and they helped me in the early days with setting up my bills and managing my money. This was all new to me. I also had to plan my time more carefully, and I was solely responsible for this. It took me much longer to do activities, so I had to factor this in when thinking about being on time for work or just leaving the flat. I remember my mother taking me food shopping, walking around the supermarket with me, and helping me find the best way to navigate my way down the food aisles with a trolley. It did take a good half of the day to do my shopping though. It wasn't easy, but it was still another achievement, and that made me feel good.

Life was good. I had a job, my own place to live, a car to drive and a collection of friends to keep me busy. Despite my sticks, I felt I was living a life similar to any able-bodied person, and more importantly, I was living a similar life to my sisters, who by now had also moved out of home, had jobs and were beginning to settle down. It was always important for me to be like my sisters. When we were growing up, my family never made me feel any different. I did everything my sisters did, so in my adult years, I didn't want this to change.

I was approaching my fifth year in employment at the college when the management told me that due to some changes, they could no longer support my role within Student Services, to do with health reasons. This upset me hugely. I had really enjoyed helping people in the way that I did in Student Services. I also loved having that close interaction with the students. It made me feel part of a crowd of able-bodied people. I enjoyed the jokes, the banter, the chatting. However, I told myself that the people making the decisions had my best interest at heart, and at least I was still working at the college.

I later discovered that the new Student Services manager who had recently joined us was the person responsible for instigating these changes and she didn't have my best interests at heart at all. The increase in work had resulted in the office being busier, with more people moving around, which was making it so much more difficult for me. This might have been why the development officer from the Shaw Trust had suggested an electric scooter, which we had proved wasn't going to work. I hadn't quite anticipated how these changes were going to impact my work, but there was no denying that they did.

It also became apparent to my parents that this manager had been trying to find reasons for me to leave my role by making a few enquiries. A good friend of my parents who worked at the college had heard these whisperings of the attempts to move me out of my role. Similarly, a colleague that my mother was working with at the time, who also had connections with the college and knew this manager, had heard similar whisperings. However, the most certain clue was a phone call that my mother received from our family doctor, who told my mother that this person wanted to have an interview with him about my health. Of course, my doctor could never agree to this, but to know that this person had asked him rang huge alarm bells.

And that was when the management told me that, for health reasons, I would have to move to a different department and a different role.

My parents told me years later how they wished they had followed this situation up with the principal of the college or with the trade unions and others of influence so that they could have tried to stop what was clearly a very unfair situation unfolding. I think it would have been hard for anyone to see what was going on, and there wasn't the support from the law in the same way there is today, in the form of the Equality Act. I wasn't being asked to leave, I was given another job, and so by all accounts at the time, it was a justified and acceptable solution. The college were still employing me, and for my family and me, we adopted the positive attitude that I would gain new skills and move further through my career. However, in hindsight, the impact that it had on me in my later years was so profound, and I wonder if I ever really regained my confidence.

In those days, there wasn't the equal rights or anti-discrimination focus that is so apparent now. Disabled people really weren't given as many opportunities, and I think there was certainly an undercurrent of discrimination around. There weren't the checks to ensure disabled people weren't being discriminated against when they applied for jobs or whilst they were currently employed in a job. The establishment of the Shaw Trust was a positive set-up to ensure disabled people had equal opportunities. The Disability Discrimination Act was introduced in 1995, but it was new and I'm not sure how much leverage my family and I would have had if we were to have pursued potential discrimination through this. The Equality Act superseded the Disability Discrimination Act in 2010, and being more established, it offered disabled people much more protection over discrimination both in and outside of the workplace. I believe that if I found myself in a similar situation today, I would have much more support and backing from the law if I was to put forward a case. But all this happened a long time ago, and submitting a complaint was not to be. We were all determined to stay focused, keep positive, keep the peace, and move forward with my career.

I was upset to move away from Student Services, but I thought, life goes on, I still had a job, and so my new role began. I was a Student Records Assistant, and I was positive about this new role. I was still working at the college but in a different location. My main duties consisted of filing, collecting the post and sending off the outgoing post. My name soon became the Post Lady. The post was a full-time job, so it kept me out of mischief! This role didn't have the same 'buzz' as Student Services did, but I knew I just had to get used to it, and quickly. The filing was particularly difficult, nearly impossible. I had to lift documents from one height to another, and then carefully place them in a drawer. Filing cabinets are typically tall, so it was particularly hard for me to lift the documents that needed filing to place them in the top drawer. Not being tall myself, and finding it hard to stand straight, was particularly challenging and I sometimes was just not able to do it. It really wasn't fair to have given me this job to do. Whether this was all part of the intention to move me out of the college completely, I'll never know, but my confidence was severely knocked.

I continued to focus on the positives of the role. I was in my early twenties, and I wanted life to be good. I had all the normal hopes and dreams that any other twenty-year-old had. I was looking forward to the future, I wanted to have a career, I could now drive, I was living independently, so I had achieved my three goals and I wanted to retain all three.

I quickly learnt a new skill: using the franking machine! Once my colleagues taught me how to use it, I was away. I just had to remember to weigh the letters and put the correct postage in the franking machine. It was quite straightforward until I had to do registered post or recorded post, for important parcels or documents that needed to arrive the next day. This was more complicated. I had to fill in paperwork just in case parcels went astray, which did happen once or twice but I was able to track the parcel by liaising with the post office and with the forms that I had filled in. This showed me that paperwork certainly has its benefits as boring as it can be to do! But how times have changed. I suspect there's not this amount of paperwork today; all the tracking is no doubt done by a computer system.

In this office, the main task was to input all the enrolment forms to the MIS (Management Information Systems). I thought I would be quite good at this as I love using computers and I could stay in one place and do this, without worrying about moving around an office too much. It would also give me some variety to the day. However, there were not enough computers, so only a few people were allowed to use the MIS and input the enrolment forms, and I wasn't one of them, unfortunately. I told myself I could keep asking, but in the meantime, I had to get on with my other tasks.

As I have mentioned, I didn't find filing easy and frankly it's also not the most exciting, or satisfying job, but someone has to do it. Why my manager thought it was the right task for me, I'll never know. Although I now wonder whether the intention was for me to find it difficult.

I had to file all the enrolment forms into filing drawers. This was incredibly hard and was a job that required me to be on my feet, balancing. Sometimes I was able to sit down and file when the filing drawers were lower down, but even that was difficult because the drawers got very compact, and I needed to lean down and use my upper body to shift the content of the drawers around to get the next form in. Even though I was sitting down, it was still difficult to lean over because I didn't have the strength in my legs to really reach down that far without feeling as if I might lose my balance and fall off the chair! My boss didn't seem to understand how hard all this was for me, filing both standing up and sitting down. I did tell her that I was finding it difficult, but the response was, 'You need to try because we're all really busy!'

I hadn't wanted to, but at this point I decided to mention the health and safety policy. Well, on hearing those words, I got a different reaction. She replied, 'Ok, leave the drawers that you can't reach.'

I felt angry that I had to draw her attention to this; she could see that I had difficulty with my mobility. I absolutely agree that it's good to give most things a go, but if it's going to cause an accident and a person just doesn't feel comfortable, then it's not worth it. We all know what our limitations are; well, I certainly did in this situation.

Sadly, I never felt part of the Student Records team. I tried so often to show an interest; I was keen to learn new skills or to help with different jobs, such as the inputting of the enrolment forms using the MIS, but I was always told that I would be shown how to do this at another time. It wouldn't have taken long to explain it to me, but everyone was too busy. I just wanted to feel part of the team and to help more. To this day, I don't really know if my disability was holding me back, meaning that I wasn't getting all the opportunities that I might have been given if I didn't have cerebral palsy. I hope this wasn't the case, but it has crossed my mind several times over the years. Or maybe I should have been more assertive, stood up for myself more, challenged why I wasn't given more training or the opportunity to learn more skills. I was just so grateful for a job, for the chance to work, for the chance to be like any able-bodied person that I didn't want to complain or give anyone any reason to not like me or to take my job away from me. In my older years looking back though, I can see that the job was totally wrong for me, and the college really should have done more to look after me and find me more appropriate work that I could do.

One day, I heard that there was a team meeting. I was keen to go along to this, hoping that I could get a better idea of what the wider team were doing. However, I had no such luck with attending this meeting; instead, my manager asked me to stay in the office and answer the phones. I felt very nervous about this because I feared I wouldn't know the answer to a question that a caller might ask me, and I didn't have access to a computer to look up the answer to any question either. I didn't even have a login to a computer, and I still struggled with writing down information whilst holding a phone.

Of course, the phone did ring eventually. Shall I answer it, I thought. The fear of being asked a question that I didn't know the answer to still prevailed, and exactly this happened. However, I took the initiative to reassure the caller that I would pass on their message, and someone would get back to them. In this situation, the caller was very understanding and was happy for someone else to contact them at another time. However, I could have been responding to a grumpy caller who might have been in a rush and could have been rude to me.

I also had to be mindful of any confidentiality and personal information issues. We always had to confirm with the caller that they were happy for us to note down their personal information, and if we did then write it down, we had to follow the standard data protection procedure before dealing with the query accordingly.

I continued to be open about not feeling part of the Student Records team, but there didn't seem to be a solution and I had to just carry on. I began to think, 'Why am I here?' I was feeling isolated, and my confidence was on a huge decline, such a change from how I felt in Student Service. It didn't feel good, and I was concerned. After some thought and after talking to various people, I asked if I could help in another office called the Directions Office. My manager agreed that this was a good idea.

So, every Thursday morning I worked in the Directions Office. Directions was similar to the YTS (Youth Training Scheme). Individuals attended the college on a day-release, and they then had the opportunity to get further training in an area of interest to them. This could range from engineering construction to food and hospitality. My job was to phone the departmental clerks of the appropriate section to see whether the individual had attended. I then could fill in the register to mark them off. I really did enjoy Thursday mornings; it was something different and gradually I was rebuilding my confidence. It was a shame it couldn't be a full-time job.

I continued to send out the post. People would come to me at the very last minute and say, 'This parcel needs to go urgently, Suz, and it needs to be recorded delivery.'

This gave me more delightful paperwork! Sometimes I found it hard to do it all by myself and once I asked for help. The manager of Student Records got cross. He said to me, 'This is your job, Suz, not anyone else's!'

'I know,' I replied, 'but I'm finding it hard doing it all on my own and the person had offered to help me, which was really kind of them.'

'Okay,' he said, 'But next time ask someone else!'

How he could have expected me, or anyone, to do it all ourselves, was beyond me. The post was building up by the minute, into a big mountain of paper and parcels. I did try to ask people to bring the post down earlier if they could, but sometimes the last-minute requests just couldn't be helped.

I was now entering my sixth year at the college, but I had been thinking for some time that I was ready to move on. I didn't feel as if I was progressing, and I'd lost that enthusiasm to come to work because I wasn't getting the same enjoyment. It wasn't the kind and empathetic environment that I had first experienced when working in Student Services, where people were mindful and sensitive to my disability.

I contacted the Shaw Trust, who helped me with my search for a new job. After about a month, I came across a vacancy for a receptionist at the Shaw Trust's head office in Trowbridge. Although Trowbridge was thirty miles away from where I lived, I thought, 'Well, I can drive, so let's go for it!' I knew the Shaw Trust well by now because they had supported me so much during my job at the college for the last six years, and given what they specialized in, I thought I probably didn't need to worry about whether the building was accessible. So, managing the work environment at the head office was a weight off my mind.

I went ahead and applied for the job. A couple of weeks

passed, and I still hadn't heard anything; all I could do was wait! Although it was frustrating waiting, it also lifted my spirits knowing that I had an opportunity of getting another job, so I began to feel happier in myself. I continued to work hard at Student Records, and to the best of my ability, whilst waiting for confirmation about the job at the Shaw Trust.

Eventually I received a letter from the Shaw Trust inviting me for an interview. I was so excited, although I knew that the hardest part was yet to come, the interview. I hadn't been in an interview since starting at the college six years ago. They made me so nervous. Also, as it was the Shaw Trust, it was likely that I would know the staff who were interviewing me, because I had been on arranged holidays with the Shaw Trust in the past, so I had mixed with quite a few of the staff in a social environment. You would think this would have made me feel more relaxed, but it made me feel more nervous. In a working environment, I would have to be professional; I had to remember this!

I can only describe it as a feeling of being on cloud nine during the week leading up to my interview. I was so pleased to have been invited to an interview, to have come this far, although I still had to get the job.

I did a recce drive to Trowbridge a couple of days before the interview so that I was familiar with the route, and so I could time the journey. My sense of direction is appalling, and the last thing that I wanted to happen was to get lost on the day of my interview. The Shaw Trust was easy to find, much to my amazement, and the drive took about an hour.

On the day of my interview, I was so nervous. I gave myself plenty of time upon arriving at the interview to sit in the car and try to relax. I went over in my head thinking of the type of questions that the interview panel might ask me, so I might have some hope of preparing and then giving the right response, or at least a good, well-thought-out one. However, you can never really know how it's going to go!

My heart was beating ten to the dozen as I entered the building. A friendly face greeted me, so I soon began to calm down. She took me to the interview room; now was my moment to convince them that I was right for the job. The questions that they asked me were standard ones, and they were questions that thankfully I had prepared for. I felt as if I answered them well, but only time would tell.

I went back to my job at the college the next day. I hadn't told anyone in the office about the interview, because if I was unsuccessful, I didn't want to have to explain this. So, when my work colleagues asked if I'd had a nice day off, I just said, 'Yes, thanks!'

The waiting felt like forever, but eventually, I heard that the Shaw Trust were offering me the job! Yippee! I immediately accepted it and now I could tell people. Some people were quite shocked that I was moving on, but I had to tell them that I was doing what I thought was best. Other people were concerned about the amount of travelling I would have to do every day; it was a sixty-mile round journey. I replied with, 'I will see how it goes. At least my car will be getting a good run on a daily basis.'

I had a bright green Peugeot 206 and I loved it!

I gave in my notice to Salisbury College as soon as I had received the written confirmation that I had the job. I remember thinking, 'Oh my days, this month is going to go so slowly!' but my last day at the college soon came around and off I went! I certainly would miss a few people. My colleagues gave me a very nice leaving present; it was very appropriate. An automatic tea maker called a Tea's Maid! All the staff used to tease me about liking my tea so much. Even though I hadn't enjoyed the last couple of years so much, I still wanted to thank both the previous management in Student Services and my current management for giving me the opportunity to experience the working environment.

So, to the Shaw Trust I went. Were they ready for me?

The day of my new job had arrived. I was so excited! I had to be at work for 8.30am, but I had to drive the thirty miles first and I feared that the traffic would be a nightmare at this time of the morning, so I left myself plenty of time. I hate being late and it would look awful to be late on the first day of my new job. Thankfully, I got to my first day of work at the Shaw Trust with plenty of time to spare.

My manager met me as I walked into the building. She soon showed me around and introduced me to everyone. They were all so friendly. I'm sure they understood that starting a new job can be really daunting. I was job sharing with a woman called Kim. She was nice and made me feel at ease. It was her first day too. I began the job by shadowing people for a couple of days, which was useful, and I was thankful that I wasn't thrown into the deep end too soon!

There was a system known as flexitime at the Shaw Trust. I hadn't heard of this before, but it was really useful and helped me manage my time according to what suited me best; so, if an employee wanted to come into work early, they could, and then they were allowed to leave early. As long as you did your allocated hours, you could fit these hours in around the daytime work hours, within reason. Kim and I were obviously both working at the reception and it suited Kim best to come in early at 8.30am, so she could leave earlier, whereas it was more convenient for me to come in a bit later and leave later. Therefore, my working day started at 10am, which meant that I missed rush hour and it just gave me that extra travelling time in the mornings, which I appreciated. There was a signing-in system to log what time you arrived and what time you left. This was primarily a safety check, so in the event of a fire it would be known who was in the building, but it was also the way in which the company knew you had been in work to work your hours, and therefore ensured that we got paid!

Alongside operating a switchboard, I also had to do the post on a daily basis. There were development officers all over the country who worked for the Trust, and they each had a pigeon-hole for their post. Twice a week I had to send out their post to wherever they were in the country. In order to work out the price of sending an item, I had to weigh it and to my frustration, there were no electronic scales to calculate the price of this postage automatically. So, I had to rely on my maths ability, by weighing the post and then calculating the price. It made the job slightly harder, and it made me think that I wish I had concentrated better in my maths lesson at school. I got there in the end, and it was good mental arithmetic practice for me!

When it got busy, there was always help for me. The atmosphere in the office and within the company was so nice because people understood about disability. You didn't have to explain why certain tasks took a little longer. In the past I had hated having to explain why I was taking so long with doing a task; it was so awkward when other people just didn't understand. Although on reflection, maybe it is hard for employers to understand how difficult it can be for someone with a disability to be part of a workforce if they have never employed a disabled person.

The first week in this new job went so quickly; it flew by! I was still very anxious when I had to answer the phone. I just couldn't get my words out. It was so embarrassing. I knew that I just needed to build up my confidence. My experiences in the previous job had knocked my confidence; it had felt like I was at the back of the class. The nature of answering a phone means that you must 'think on your feet', which made me nervous, just as it had in my previous job. I so desperately wanted to make a good impression, but the more I felt I had to make a good impression the more nervous I became.

On one occasion, I answered a call from the managing director of the Shaw Trust. When I realised who it was, I just froze. I tried so hard to get my words out, but they just didn't come; nothing happened, no words, just a faint stutter. I felt so ashamed of myself, so deflated that I couldn't do this when it really mattered. I spoke to my boss, who was very understanding and supportive. She suggested ways that could help me with this issue. We came to an agreement that I would practice calling people internally. This would allow me to make a note of how I felt and how I got on after the call, and it gave me a safe environment to practice speaking on the phone because the people I was calling understood what I was trying to achieve. I didn't have to worry about my role in Reception; this was being covered by Kim, and there was also another lady, who I had shadowed when I first started the job, who was willing to help us out whilst I tried to combat this anxiety over answering the phone. There were plenty of other tasks to do, and I still found shredding therapeutic, satisfying, and bizarrely relaxing, so I helped with this. I also enjoyed typing, so there were times when people would give me notes to type up. I also continued with managing the post for the Trust, both internally and externally. So, I kept busy, and my days were filled up quickly.

After a month of being in the job, I still didn't feel comfortable answering the phone. I would try so hard to keep calm and give it a go, but every time I would tumble into a dialogue of stuttering and pausing, followed by more stuttering; it felt irrecoverable. I just wished I didn't have the problem. I remember on one occasion, I needed to call a company to ask for some information. They then asked me for an address, but I just couldn't say the words. Eventually, the person put the phone down on me. I think they thought I was mucking around so I never got the information I requested, all because of this stutter.

The travelling of sixty miles every day was beginning to take its toll on me. The nights were getting darker, and the roads were icy. It was a particularly bad road to travel on, especially in the dark. Before I accepted the job, my friends and family had suggested that I move closer to the place of work, to reduce the travelling time. But I loved where I was living, so I didn't consider it an option. I also didn't want the pressure of starting a new job and moving at the same time. I was only able to focus on one thing at a time.

Another month passed and I noticed that people were asking me whether I was feeling alright. I must admit, I did wonder why they kept asking. Even my manager took me aside one day and asked how I was getting on.

'I love the people here,' I told her. 'They have been so supportive. But I am finding parts of the job difficult. Particularly answering the phone, and to be honest, I am now finding the travelling tiring.'

It was also dawning on me how the previous job at the college had knocked my confidence. I had ended up just feeling part of the background there, with no challenge. In this new job, where I was working on the reception and being part of the 'front line', I needed the confidence, and I felt I just didn't have it anymore. I had no idea this would happen, that I would feel this way.

I eventually decided I needed a change, I needed to try something else; something that was more suited to me and to my skills. A job that would rebuild my confidence and one that would require less travel. The Shaw Trust agreed to support me on my hunt for another job nearer home. I was extremely grateful for their understanding.

It was back to the drawing board, as the saying goes. However, I was quite sure about one thing; I didn't want to be a receptionist again. I wanted to do something that involved computers, such as data inputting or even web designing; although I would need to get a qualification in web design if I wanted to pursue this. I had already achieved a qualification for data inputting.

I visited my local job centre weekly, looked in the job section of the papers and regularly browsed the internet. I ensured my CV was up to date, and I sent it out to various companies. The job centre also put me in touch with a DEA (Disability Employment Adviser). I was sure that having the support of a DEA would make the difference; working with the DEA and the Shaw Trust would surely help me find the right job.

But it wasn't going well. Even with the help that I was getting. I continued sending letters directly to companies that I would like to work for, but I didn't get a response. I wondered if I just didn't fit the job criteria or the job description and this was why I didn't get an interview, or whether it was because I had a disability. I noticed that every job vacancy that was advertised had an 'equal opportunities' tick next to it. I understood that this meant that providing the candidate fitted the job criteria, they would go for an interview, regardless of whether they had a disability or not, which was really promising to read and positive for me.

I continued to visit the job centre on a weekly basis and after six months of being on the Job Seekers Allowance, I was told that I had to go on a work placement programme, which meant that I didn't have to continue to go into the job centre on a weekly basis. Yippee! Going on the work placement programme would get me back into a routine of getting up earlier in the morning, mixing with people, and getting on with the day, all of which I wanted to do.

The hope was that following the work placement, the company would offer me a permanent job. To me, these work placements sounded like an excellent idea if they had the potential to lead to a permanent position. I really enjoyed most of my work placements that I did, and by being in the loop of the working life, I could gradually feel my confidence return.

My first placement was at the local hospital. I worked in the Medical Records Department doing data input and various other tasks. I worked there for six months on a part-time basis. Unfortunately, it didn't lead to a permanent job, but it was a great experience and one that I could add to my CV.

However, it did leave me back looking for a job again, until another placement opportunity became available. Eventually, I got an interview to be a data entry clerk. It was back at the hospital, which was good. I prepared by going through a few mock interviews that the job centre organised for me. I had good feedback and the interviewer told me that the mock interviews went well.

The day finally arrived for the real interview; I was feeling positive. I felt as if I answered all the questions well, but at the end of the interview, I had to do a test on data entry. Unfortunately, I didn't finish it in the time that I had been given, so I was sure I wouldn't be successful, and my intuition proved to be correct. A couple of days later I was told that I didn't get the job. It did upset me because the job had seemed promising and one that I would enjoy. Anyway, I told myself that I just had to keep going, but I was now beginning to wonder what I was doing wrong in the interviews. So, on this occasion, I did ask for some feedback on the interview. They simply told me that the other candidates had more experience. This wasn't really very helpful.

Therefore, another work placement loomed. It was at a pension company, working in a department called Annual Review, and it was a part-time position. The role included data inputting and helping to collate booklets. For this, I had to use a binding machine, which I found difficult because my coordination is not very good. I tried to work as quickly as possible, but still, my manager said, 'Suz, you need to be quicker!'

I told him I was finding it difficult, but he wasn't listening and had no sympathy. I thought he was being particularly harsh, especially as the company were not paying me to do this work!

I went back to the job centre and said I was finding this placement physically difficult. Unfortunately, they weren't much help, and the response was to continue with the placement. So, I did.

On completion of the work placement, I was told that there wouldn't be a permanent position available for me; to be honest, I wasn't that upset! A few months later, my twin sister, Pippa, got a job at the same pension company. Of course, I was happy for her, but it did make me wonder if they didn't employ me because I was too slow. I never found out if this was the case. They did tell me that they enjoyed having me work for them, which was nice at least.

By now, I was at my whit's end, wondering if I would ever get a job. I was under pressure from the job centre to apply for jobs, and some of them were not even in buildings that were accessible for me; there was no law to provide disabled access in those days. However, I had to apply for these jobs regardless of my concerns, and on quite a few occasions, I didn't even get a response.

When I started work at the college, in 1992, unemployment was rising and it reached a peak of 10.7% in 1993, so I was very lucky to get a job when I did. However, the unemployment rate went steadily down, and by 2005 it hit a low of 4.7% before beginning to rise again. Given these statistics, I should have had a better chance of finding a job, given that the unemployment figure was on the decline during the time that I was trying to find employment. However, it was not to be. I really did feel that my disability was acting against me, and this made me feel very low. It was a continuous uphill struggle.

The job centre then advised me that I had to do another training course, mainly to help me with my interviewing techniques and job searching skills. Well, the first day was an absolute washout. I was the only disabled person there, and the classroom was on the first floor and there was no lift. I physically couldn't walk up the stairs, and it would have been dangerous to try. When I voiced my difficulty, the course administrator told me that I could do my work in the computer room downstairs, on my own! Occasionally a tutor would come and ask if I needed any help.

I continued with the course for a couple of weeks, but the situation remained; me working on my own in a room downstairs when the rest of the course attendants were upstairs, talking and sharing experiences. I must admit to feeling that it was a little pointless for me to be downstairs on my own whilst everyone else was upstairs. I was supposed to be learning and interacting with people, but I couldn't do this because the building wasn't accessible for me. So, I asked if I could do the work at home, on my own computer, and then email it across at the end of the day when I had completed it.

'No!' the powers that be told me.

I thought this was so unfair! More than unfair. I had a genuine reason why I couldn't join in with the other people on the course, and I was trying to compromise with them by making suggestions of different ways of working. I wasn't being listened to, so I walked out in the end, but this resulted in my job seeker allowance money being terminated. It was a bad course, badly administered and took no account of a person with a disability.

After a few weeks, the training course administrator invited me back on to the training course with the promise that they would run the course in a room downstairs. Why they didn't think of this in the first place, when they realised how much I was struggling, is beyond me. Anyway, I did go back, and I did meet some nice people. Being downstairs was much better, however, I'm not sure the course taught me much. I didn't feel I came away with better job searching skills or a better interview technique. But at least I had tried.

Whilst I was job searching one day, a tutor said, 'Suz, I think this job would suit you.'

I looked at the job description. It was a role as a medical records assistant, working for a mental health trust in the NHS, and it was locally based, so I wouldn't have the issue of a long drive again. I agreed, this did look like a job that I would enjoy, so I went straight ahead and applied for it, although there were a couple of things that I was hesitant about. The job was temporary, and it wasn't clear how long for, and I was looking for a permanent job. Also, my fear of answering the phone crept back in, and I became worried that I would have to do this. However, I still went ahead and applied for it; I knew I had to try. I still had an issue with using the telephone, due to a lack of confidence, but I was trying hard to overcome this. After I had applied, all I could do was sit back and wait to see if I would get an interview.

Which I did! When they called to tell me and to arrange the interview with me, I thought I was dreaming! But it was all true. I was over the moon; it had been so long since something positive had happened to me.

I brushed up again on my interviewing technique, as it had been a while since I had been to an interview. I just prayed that I would do well on the day.

The day of the interview arrived, and I felt quietly positive. I just had a feeling that I would nail this interview! It helped that friendly people greeted me when I walked into the building. The Medical Records supervisor met me first, and then took me across to the interview room, where she introduced me to another woman who managed the medical records throughout the whole trust. She worked in Bristol mainly but came to Salisbury regularly; the trust had offices all around Wiltshire.

I thought that the interview went well. All of the usual questions, which I had prepared for. They told me that the job would be for three months initially. I left the interview feeling even more positive, knowing that all I had to do now was sit and wait for the outcome. I felt nervous all day, with that butterfly feeling in my tummy. I didn't have to wait long. I got a call that evening. They offered me the job! I couldn't believe it. I was ecstatic! I accepted the job without any hesitation.

I had to go through a check by the Criminal Record Bureau, and I was required to have a medical. This all took about another six weeks to complete; I could hardly wait!

Whilst I waited, I spoilt myself and bought some new clothes. I had received a clothing allowance from the job centre, which was a great help. Now that I had a job, I also had to sort out my situation regarding benefits. Initially, the benefits department said that I would be worse off financially now that I was going to be working and not receiving benefits. My instant response was, 'Surely you should be encouraging me to work, not discouraging me!'

After the job centre had done a back-to-work calculation for me, it turned out that financially, working was better for me. I knew that on a social level it would be fantastic because I love being around people.

The start day arrived, so it was all systems go! There were two other people in the office; one was my supervisor, and the other person was a woman who worked part-time. Naturally, it did take me a while to settle in, but everyone was so nice and supportive, and Radio 2 was always playing quietly in the office.

I had to go through some training before being able to operate the computer system. This training was in Bristol, for just the day. On this occasion, rather than driving, I arranged for the Link scheme in my area to drive me, which they willingly did. The Link scheme is part of a 'community first' set-up. It is a volunteer-led service that aims to improve the quality of life for disadvantaged, elderly or disabled people. It helps them access important local services if they are not able to get there themselves using either their own transport or by public transport. I just wasn't comfortable driving to a place where I had never been before, let alone a town that I had never driven through. The training went well, and when I returned to the office the next day I felt as if I could really get stuck into the job, which involved archiving and retrieving medical records for the trust.

I was able to get a comfortable chair on the Access to Work scheme, and they gave me a trolley to help me carry around items. Unfortunately, the trolley didn't offer the desired assistance due to my balance and coordination being poor. I couldn't put the brakes of the trolley on quick enough, which left it hurtling into various unsuspecting office furniture! Needless to add, I wouldn't be pushing a trolley again!

However, my confidence was returning, and I was buzzing! Life for me was sweet. This job was different from my previous roles. Obviously, I had to get the work done, which I did to the best of my ability, but I didn't feel the constant pressure of people looking over my shoulder. If I knew I was unable to finish a job on my own, I could ask for help and didn't feel nervous about this, as I had in previous jobs. It was all part of working for a good team and working together to help and support each other. I still liked shredding – it was strangely therapeutic and satisfying – so I made sure my colleagues knew this; I often offered to do this when no one else wanted to.

After I had been in the job for over a year, they extended my contract, which was fine by me! However, there had been many changes within the trust over the years, and changes to the job descriptions. My manager told me that my job would also include helping to archive the medical files, as well as inputting and retrieving them to and from the system. The medical files had previously been stored with Pickford's, but it made sense to have them closer, which is why the archiving moved to our site. This is what drove the change to my job description, and it meant that I would now have to help to archive them. I knew that this change was inevitable as my supervisor had told me about it when I was first appointed the job; it had just been a question of time. I loved this job so much, but physically it was going to be impossible for me to do the archiving and therefore I soon realised I wouldn't be able to continue. It would be too physically demanding, requiring me to do tasks I just couldn't do. Life is unfair! And it was happening all over again. The company was moving me out of a job into another role that I physically could not do. I was being given little choice but to leave, and my confidence was taking another knock. But I had to try and move on. I told myself that at least I'd had the opportunity to work at a place I loved, doing a job that I loved, and for longer than was originally anticipated.

I thought it would be easy to get another job because of the experience that I had gained over the years. My CV wasn't looking too bad, I had done a number of training courses in my previous roles, which I hoped would help. But, oh no, it wasn't easy.

I returned to the job centre to ask for help, and I had decided that I wanted a change in career direction. In hindsight, maybe I should have continued in the career path that I had been part of for the last ten years – administrative and computer work – but I figured that this would inherently involve answering the phone at some point, and I now had a real problem with this. Maybe I should have requested professional, psychological help. My sister Rose tried some hypnotherapy with me, specifically focusing on my stuttering, and trying to make me feel calm when I answered the phone; however, we weren't having regular sessions, and it probably wasn't the best idea to seek this type of professional help within the family. I think also, that in those days, people weren't so aware of the holistic therapies being promoted to help with these types of anxieties. I didn't know what was available, but maybe I didn't look hard enough. Visiting my GP to ask for specialist help with stuttering felt a step to far, but in hindsight, maybe I should have. I just don't think I knew how to overcome the stuttering or what options of help were available, and so the phobia around answering the phone remained.

So, I went with my decision to change career. I wanted to work with children. By now, my sisters had children; I had nieces and nephews, and I just loved being around them. I could see that it was often demanding working with children, but I also knew how rewarding it is.

I began to tell people about my idea, about my ambitions, but I could hear the hesitation in their voices. People said, 'It's really hard, Suz. What would you do if a child had fallen over? Would you be able to physically help them?'

I understood what they were saying, but I wanted to have a go, to understand the extent of my abilities to work with children. You don't know until you've tried. I also had to give it a go just to know whether I really did want to have this type of job.

I spent a couple of weeks on a work placement at a holiday playscheme for school-aged children, based at our local hospital. I was there just to help and interact with the children. There were obviously other staff around to assist me with any of the physical elements of the job that I couldn't do. It was interesting to see the curiosity from the children when they saw me. What is beautiful about children is that they will just say or ask what is on their minds. As a child, you don't have to think it through; you just say it!

'Why do you have sticks?' the children often asked me.

'Because I have poorly legs,' I would reply.

The next question was, 'Why?'

'Some people are just different,' I would reply.

'Oh!' the children would say, still with that look of concern and curiosity on their faces.

I didn't mind their questions at all. I welcomed them! I was beginning to feel that the children were warming to me now, accepting me. I would often read to them or play games with them! I really did enjoy my time at the play scheme.

The hospital also had a nursery, which ran during term time and holiday time, so I also did some voluntary work there. Again, I loved it! Reading, playing and interacting with the children. It gave me such a buzz; I found the children so interesting. One day, a child asked me to go into the shed to help them get a toy.

'I'm afraid I can't get up the step,' I said, as I tried to lift my leg up onto the step, but with no luck; the step was too high.

So, the child proceeded to show me and told me how easy it was and that I should try again. Just then, the whistle sounded. I was 'saved by the whistle' as the nursery workers told the children to go back inside. But I was smiling like a Cheshire cat for the rest of the day!

My voluntary work ended after a few months, but it had certainly been beneficial to have the experience. I did realise that it was hard work, but it really was so rewarding at times too. My aim was still to work with children; I hadn't been put off in the slightest! But I did understand that due to my disability, working with older children would be the better route. I loved working with the younger children too, but I did agree that it was a bit of a concern that if they needed physical help, I wouldn't always be able to offer this. The next step would be to gain an official qualification in childcare, so I could take on more work. I never did pursue this, but there is time yet!

I continued to consider other career options. With the rise and development of the Internet, I become increasingly interested in web design. I enjoyed looking at the presentation of a website and how the designer had chosen to make it look, and how clever it was to navigate easily through the different web pages. I realised that if it wasn't straightforward and obvious how to find the way around a website, it would put people off that website, so I could appreciate the importance of a good website design. I loved all the bright colours – this really attracted me to a website.

So, I set myself a challenge. I wanted to learn how to build my own website. When I told people about my idea, they did warn me that I would find it hard, but I still wanted to give it a go. I often reflect that when I get a negative response like this, it encourages me to work even harder to achieve it. It's my stubborn personality setting in!

I began the search for an 'open-learning' online web-designer course, that I could do in my own time. I eventually found what looked to be a good course, so I went ahead and contacted the course providers. Shortly after, one of the tutors contacted me to make an appointment with me, to have a chat about what I wanted to achieve.

A couple of days later we met, and the tutor explained what the course entailed. I reminded him that I was a complete beginner, and he suggested I start with a programme called FrontPage. I had heard of it but had never worked with it, so I was now excited to get going.

It didn't take me long to enrol on the course. It was expensive but I really wanted to do this. The course provider gave me books to work through and I had a tutor who was in regular contact with me, offering advice and support. I was stuck into it straight away. Thankfully there were no exams as part of the course (phew, I didn't consider myself someone who was very comfortable with exams). Instead, my tutor told me that once I had finished an assignment, I should mail it across to him, and he would mark it and give me feedback. Feedback is always good – it gives you the direction for improvement. Without any feedback, I might have thought that I was the best! But no one can be the best – there is always room for improvement, and I kept this in mind all through the course.

After I had handed in my last assignment, I waited patiently for my final mark, for the results. They took a little while to come through, but eventually, a white envelope made its way into my letterbox, my results contained within. I was so nervous, shaking as I picked up the envelope. But I didn't need to worry – I had passed. I had achieved it!

I could add this to my CV and show potential employers that I could build a website. To complement my new skill, I went straight on to train myself in another web design package. I hit Dreamweaver head-on!

However, I did come to realise that finding a job as a web designer was hard. Technology changes every day! I did manage to build my own website, which I was proud of, and rested with the thought that even if I'd never get a job as a web designer, then at least I could keep it as a hobby.

Finding employment generally can be one big struggle for us all, but having a disability does make it that much harder, I think; well, I felt that it did for me. I think society is changing and employers are becoming increasingly more understanding, and there are now certain laws to prevent discrimination, and there are now human rights acts that companies have to abide by. Regulations also now insist that buildings are accessible for disabled people. But, for me at the time, it was soul-destroying when the various letters arrived, over the years, to tell me, 'Sorry, on this occasion you have been unsuccessful.'

If I'm honest, I began to lose interest in looking for work. I had changed direction within my career; I had moved away from clerical work, which is what I trained in first. I had lost my confidence in this area of work. The experience at the college and the manager moving me from a job that I thought I was good at had left its mark. Similarly, the numerous times that I had been asked to do filing when it was clearly so difficult for me had also put me off working in an office. My stutter had become much worse over the years, and I hadn't managed to get on top of this, so answering the phone became a persistent problem, along with the fact that I found it very difficult to take notes whilst also holding the phone. These physical challenges were hard for me due to my disability, and because I felt like I couldn't overcome them, I averted being put in the same situation again. I then changed career direction because I was keen to pursue a career in either childcare or web design, but I couldn't find any job opportunities, and I probably needed to gain more training in both before applying for jobs should I have found them. It felt as if I had come to a dead end, and I didn't know how to turn around.

It was also a frustrating time of my life because I saw my sisters were moving on with their lives, getting married, starting a family, being employed, and so it was the first time in my life that

I noticed that my disability seemed to be preventing me from having the same opportunities as them and being like them. This had always been important to me.

I always tried to pull myself back together, regain that positivity that had been part of my life for so long, but maybe I had one knock back too many, and I just couldn't see the way forward. Interestingly, looking back at old school reports when I was writing the 'School Days' chapter, I notice that the teachers did warn that I had a fear of failure, which impacted my self-worth and self-esteem: '*There is need to build up Suzie's self-esteem and self-worth. It is her fear of failure that affects her learning now.*' Maybe there was an element of this going on for me as I was coming to terms with not finding a job. But what Treloars were telling me, was that I shouldn't fear failure, or even perceive my setbacks as failure, and that I shouldn't let it impact my confidence. They were encouraging me to keep going, to believe in myself.

I haven't been employed since, and the following years of unemployment did bring me down, down to a very low point in my life, where I really did struggle with life in general. But, as I will discuss in the next chapter, I realised I needed help. I do not regard that as a weakness but more a way of circumnavigating an obstacle.

Before moving on to the next chapter of my life, let me include the poem I wrote about 'Working Life'.

Working Life

Leaving school was cool
Now what was I going to do
Enrol on a college course
I felt excited but nervous too
"The RSA Diploma Course" is what I will do
I hope it will help me find a job too

But before that I have a lot of work to do.

The assignments keep coming through
They are interesting and keep me busy too
All my dreams came true, I passed the course
I met the examiner too.

My "Working Life" begins
I am working at the college I studied in
Student Services is exciting
With lots of people coming in
And asking questions on the types of courses the college is running
I hand them a prospectus so they can see

"Careers Advisors" worked closely with me
I booked people in the diary for them to see
Everyone was so friendly and looked after me.

It's time to move on to something new
Working with children is what I want to do
Voluntary work will give me a clue
It will train me too.

"The Play Scheme" is where I start
Some children are doing art
It's fun to see their imaginations run free
Their pictures are bright and happy
The room is filled with fun activities
It's great to see.

Working in a playgroup is the next step for me
The children are as cute as can be
They ask "Why can't I walk properly"
I say "My legs are poorly"

So I need sticks to walk you see
They all walk together
And say "Look it's easy"

The children were great with me
I enjoyed their company
It was "Lovely Juvly"
The wonderful experience will always stay with me.

Chapter 8

My struggle

Being out of work for so long did begin to have an impact on me. I very much missed being in regular contact with work colleagues and seeing them daily. My confidence had been severely knocked, first due to being moved out of jobs that I had been really enjoying, and then trying to seek work when I didn't have a job. I really tried to find another job. The job centre had enrolled me, and I started submitting my CV to various companies. I also went for a few interviews. But to no avail. It was so frustrating because the longer I was out of work, the more my confidence dropped. It felt like a catch-22 situation.

Many of my friends had moved out of the adjacent flats within the warden-assisted accommodation that I was living in. As they moved out, older people moved in. They were all very nice, but I was a young woman, still in my thirties, and I wanted to be around people my own age. I think this change in my living environment and the situation with my unemployment all began to weigh me down and dampen my spirits. My parents had offered to buy me a new property that they would adapt to accommodate my disability, but at the time I was resistant to change and was worried that it would not be a change for the better. I was also familiar with the small town that I was living in, so I didn't take them up on this offer and made the decision to stay where I was.

It was around this time that I decided to stop driving. I had been freely behind the wheel of a car from 1992 to 2009. I stopped driving in 2009 because it became too stressful for me; my depth and spatial perception on the road were deteriorating, and I didn't feel safe anymore. Everyone seemed to be in such a rush, which made me feel stressed and anxious. I also developed a paranoia that I would cause an accident, specifically that I would knock a cyclist off their bike. The space between my car and them always felt so narrow, I felt sure I would hit them. I sometimes worried that I had hit them after I had driven by, even though rationally, I knew I hadn't as I would have noticed. I just felt it was safer and easier to hand back my car.

However, I must add that learning to drive and having a driving licence when I was younger gave me so much independence in a way that was liberating and necessary. It gave me the feeling that I could do what other able-bodied people could do; that I wasn't being held back by my disability. I was thankful that I learnt to drive, that I was given the opportunity, and, over the years, to have a few awesome cars to drive!

My friends and family were concerned that I would lose much of my independence by not having a car; however, I was given some extra financial benefits to help me fund the cost of taxis and public transport to allow me to get out and about, so I still had independence to a large degree, and in my mind, I was safer. However, in hindsight, my friends and family were probably right to a certain extent, as I think it did create restrictions on both my social life but more so my employment options. It also meant that I relied more on my family and friends visiting me as I couldn't as easily get to them. I did use public transport on occasions, but it wasn't always easy getting on and off a bus, and I was of course restricted by timings and location. So, on other occasions I would book taxis using the allowance that I was given to help me with travel. But again, it wasn't always straightforward booking taxis with the room to take a wheelchair as they were limited numbers and so they weren't always available, and of course, it did get expensive. However, giving up driving was a decision I made, based on ensuring my own safety and the safety of others, and I still think it was the right thing to do.

When I look back now at what I had already achieved in those previous years, I know that I should be proud. And I should continue to be proud because despite not finding work again and discontinuing the driving, I still live independently to this day. However, back then, when I lost the opportunity to work, I felt incredibly low. I couldn't see beyond my unemployment. At the time, it felt as if the three aims that I had set myself, and that I had achieved, were now beginning to fall out of my grasp, and this was beginning to have a detrimental effect on both my mental and physical health.

Just before Christmas, in 2008, I came down with the flu. My throat was sore, and I ached, which soon gave way to a high fever and temperature. Initially, when I just had the sore throat, I tried to carry on with my daily routine; swimming, shopping when I needed to and just getting out, hoping the virus would pass. However, as the days went on, I felt worse and worse.

I had been into town one day and as I got off the bus, I thought, 'I don't think I can make it home.' I felt so dizzy. Walking wasn't easy for me at the best of times; even when I'm feeling on top of the world, but on this occasion I really did feel quite unwell. However, I had no other choice than to try to carry on, despite just wanting to curl up. I got home eventually and went straight to bed. The next day when I woke up, I felt even worse and I didn't have any appetite, which was so unlike me. I realised that I probably just needed to rest and spend a couple of days in bed, then I would feel a bit better and get my appetite back. In the end, I did decide to call the doctor, just to make sure.

I had a home visit, and they confirmed that it was flu and that I just needed to rest.

I slowly began to recover from the flu, but with my immune system already being so low, it wasn't long before I contracted another cold virus and I began to feel awful all over again, having thought that maybe I was finally getting better.

Christmas and the New Year had been and gone, and I spent most of it in bed. I had no energy and all I wanted to do was sleep. I wasn't eating and I just didn't feel hungry. I was thirsty a lot of the time, so I kept the cups of tea going. I was getting weaker every day, and I soon couldn't walk with my sticks. When I was unable to sit up due to feeling so weak, I began to realise that this was not normal. The symptoms of the flu had subsided by now, so I knew that this wasn't the problem. I also had chronic pain in my stomach. I was eventually admitted to the hospital for tests because the pain got so bad; however, none of the results were conclusive of any serious abdominal problem, despite the pain remaining. I stayed in hospital for nearly a month. The doctors initially discharged me only a week after they had admitted me, but my parents felt that this was too soon, and requested that I stay in hospital. I needed proper aftercare to be in place before I went home, as I was now very weak, and this aftercare hadn't been set up.

I still had no desire to eat. Before becoming ill with the flu, I had been a good weight, possibly a little overweight, so as I saw my weight shedding, I became keen to keep the weight down. I eventually came out of hospital in February 2009, but still with no diagnosis of what the pain in my stomach and abdomen had been. Over the next six months it became clear that I had developed a problem surrounding eating. I lost more and more weight, and with that, I lost more and more energy, but I just could not find the sensation within me of feeling hungry.

It was a confusing time for me, and I soon realised that I couldn't get myself better on my own. I needed help with the issue I now had around food and eating, so I agreed to see various therapists in the mental health profession. This was particularly difficult because my last place of employment was working at the very place where I was now a patient. It was heartbreaking when I realised that people didn't recognize me because I had lost so much weight.

Friends and family continued to encourage me to have very small amounts of food to propel my body into feeling hungry again. But in my head, I just didn't want to eat, and if I didn't feel hungry then this gave me my own reason to not eat.

My doctor asked if I was depressed and offered me a course of antidepressants, but this didn't feel like the right solution for me. I wasn't happy, but I didn't consider myself clinically depressed. My mind kept telling me that since being ill with the flu and the chronic stomach pains I had lost my appetite and the sensation of feeling hungry; therefore, I didn't need to eat. The irrational part of my mind was telling me that I only needed to eat if I felt hungry. However, if I'm honest, there was an element of feeling better about myself and my appearance because I had lost weight. I really didn't want to go back to the weight that I was.

It took me a while to admit that I had an eating disorder. I became so weak, that I was even scared to go to sleep. When people saw me, they would comment on how thin I looked. These comments evoked mixed emotions. It felt like a compliment being told that I was thin, but I knew that what I was doing to myself wasn't healthy. I just couldn't find a way to start eating properly again.

My sisters texted me every morning to ask how I was. I also had carers who came to see me every day as this was still part of the care plan that social services had put in place when I left the hospital earlier in the year. The carers were very kind; they would make me a drink and help me shower.

I continued to see my doctor on a regular basis. She was very understanding and supportive; however, it came to the stage where I needed to go into a specialized hospital as an inpatient to start some type of recovery. I felt ashamed of myself that I couldn't get better on my own, but I had tried so hard.

The doctors arranged for me to spend some time in hospital. I was encouraged to look around it first before making the final decision, so my twin, Pips, drove the sixty miles to make my first visit. We both cried on the way there.

'At least I'm getting the help that I need now. I will be alright,' I said to Pips.

We arrived at the hospital. I was so tired and weak. The staff were all so nice and caring, and I knew they just wanted me to get better, without judging me. This meant so much to me. We spent about two hours looking around the five-bedroom unit. On the way back home, I had already made my decision that I had to admit myself to this hospital. By now, I felt so ill; I could hardly keep my eyes open, and I felt so floppy. I now couldn't do any daily tasks on my own.

So, in December 2009, nearly a year after I had been ill with the flu, I accepted the offer to go to Southmead's Hospital in Bristol as an inpatient, to get the help I so desperately needed. My sisters Pips and Rose drove me back to the unit a couple of days after I had looked around it. On the journey there, I had many thoughts going around in my head whilst I closed my eyes. I was scared, nervous and apprehensive. I had never been in a unit before that dealt with this illness. I was quite far away from my family, but I had to do this, and they understood. It was going to be a difficult journey. The illness was much harder to deal with than my cerebral palsy, which is quite a statement to make.

As soon as I arrived, the carers and nurses introduced me to the other patients and the staff. The nurses didn't wear uniforms, which I thought was nice. It created a much more relaxed and less clinical atmosphere.

I was the only one in a wheelchair, and I wasn't sure how

people were going to react to this. Soon after I arrived, before I had even had time to adjust to this new environment, the care staff showed me the dining room. A nurse told me that this was where we would have meals and snacks.

It was a very controlled environment during both meal and snack times. The nurses had pre-warned me about this, but to be there, see it and experience it, was daunting. I understand now that it had to be this way. My whole life had become about food and my will to eat as little as possible. The only way around this was to change my relationship with food to get myself better. I needed help to do this, and I realised that providing a controlled environment that dictated when and what to eat is a therapy that works for many sufferers.

The medical staff told me that every hot drink I had must have milk in it, and we had to eat a snack. Everyone had a set amount of time to eat and there always had to be two members of staff at the table with us. The other inpatients would sit at the table too, but they would often finish before me. We were all at different stages in our recovery. I found it uncomfortable if they had all finished but had to wait for me before they could go. I had not eaten much food for months, so I found it very, very hard to eat. I felt full after just a drink because my stomach was still adjusting to digesting anything. If I hadn't finished the drink or snack after the allocated time, I had to stay behind and drink a mixture that had all the required nutrients in it. I had to do this on a couple of occasions. As the days went on, it did get easier. The nurses weighed me twice a week, which I hated. I wasn't allowed a drink before the weigh-in.

After some time of just having nutritional shakes and small snacks, the nurses moved me on to eating meals. They gave me a menu, specifically catered for my height. This would allow me to gain weight slowly and in the right way. They also gave me more time to eat meals, but it was still timed and the same rule applied:

if I hadn't finished, I had to have the vitamin drink, which tasted disgusting.

After every meal or snack, the nurses observed me for a certain amount of time. It felt that all I did was eat and snack all day long. There was a variety of snacks, and I could not have the same snack more than twice a week, to ensure a varied diet and to stop me from choosing the foods that I thought would be the least in calories. I didn't like this rule; however, I wanted to get better, so I followed it. If on the days that I was weighed it was noticed that I hadn't gained weight, then another type of food was added to my menu. For example, cereal or toast. This continued for all the time that I was there. I was petrified of gaining weight though, so the emotions were very conflicting; I wanted to get better, but I didn't want to gain weight.

I still don't know very much about anorexia, other than how it made me feel. I don't know why I fell victim to it. I can only assume it was a multitude of factors. Interestingly, I have read that it is possibly associated with both preterm birth and neonatal issues, and gastrointestinal issues. I have been through both of these. I don't know what the relationship is between preterm birth or neonatal issues and anorexia, and it would take quite a bit more research on my behalf to understand this, and I don't think this contributed to what I experienced. However, I can relate to the deeper, subconscious connection between gastrointestinal issues and anorexia. Following my persistent abdominal pain, which eventually resulted in the doctor admitting me to hospital, the professionals thought that it could be due to my digestive system being somewhat inactive because I wasn't eating much. With cerebral palsy, it is particularly important to keep all my muscles active. If I stop moving my muscles, they can quickly become stiff and rigid. The digestive system is full of muscles, and by not eating, I was not activating my system regularly; therefore, it was struggling to work efficiently. With what little I did eat, my digestive system would have to become active, but this caused me pain because it was like moving a stiff muscle every time I ate. So, it was quite possible that my subconscious mind was making an irrational association, telling me that if I ate, it would cause me pain, so don't eat.

I don't know this to be true, but I do know that my reluctance to eat came about after the flu because I had lost my appetite, I was not eating and therefore my digestive system slowed right down. Whether this caused the abdominal pain, I can't be sure, but I think my mind had already begun to associate abdominal pain with eating, which only amplified the problem. A self-perpetuating cycle.

There are other known perpetuating cycles of not eating. The basic one is that as you stop eating, you then lose your appetite and you don't feel the desire to eat, and therefore you don't eat. But because of not eating, several physiological changes begin to take place, such as a change to metabolism, a change to the neuroendocrine system that affects hormone release, and many more subtle changes associated with the intricate connections within the human body. I don't have the knowledge to expand further on this; however, I think it is right to make the point that although it might be thought that anorexia is a psychological illness, the physiological and hormonal changes that accompany a significant reduction in calorie intake also contribute to the illness, making it even harder to overcome. These physiological changes can cause mind-altering thinking, due to prolonged depleted nutrition, so that a person is no longer able to rationalise or reason with their reality. Added to all of this, is the simple, and obvious change in your body weight, which if you have wanted to lose weight, comes as a welcomed change, and one that I wanted to continue with.

The other more well-known causes of anorexia are lack of control over your life, loneliness and low self-esteem, depression and even a tendency towards obsessive compulsive disorder (OCD). Whilst I never felt as if I was depressed or lonely at the time, I can see that I might have been experiencing a lack of control and low self-esteem, given how I was unable to find employment and my life seemed to have gone from one extreme to another. I had gone from living, working and driving in a similar way to any able-bodied person, to becoming acutely aware of my disability by my inability to find employment. I wasn't consciously aware that this would have led to an eating disorder, but I doubt it helped. I also suffer from an element of OCD. I think this began to emerge when I became slightly obsessive around the fear that I had knocked down a cyclist whilst driving my car. I would go over it repeatedly if there was the possibility that I could have done this and not realised.

Whatever the cause of this illness, it was with me, and it was very real, for this period of my life. Despite the complexities and unknowns surrounding it, I knew that I desperately needed to get better and to deal with it, so that I could try to regain my independence.

The clinic at Bristol dealt very well with the physical impact of the anorexia, by using this controlled and strict approach to an eating routine, and it wasn't long before I was gaining the required weight. Although I wasn't sure how I felt about this, I had no choice. However, there was clearly the emotional aspect to this illness. The nurses were lovely and tried to help me to navigate my way through my emotions, whilst trying to explain what they understood about the condition. I used to have many chats with them. They had training in understanding people with this illness, so they would often reassure me that I wasn't alone. We weren't offered official counselling as such; it was more informal, with the option of a one-to-one conversation if we needed it. I do remember the nurses asking questions such as, 'Why are you afraid of food?' My answer was always, 'I don't want to put on weight.'

After a lot of help, both physically and mentally, I finally managed to eat the food on the menu specifically suggested for me in the allocated time without it being too much of an ordeal. At this point, I began to think that I was getting better and getting back on the right track.

After a month and a half of being at the unit, I finally could stand up using my sticks. When I had arrived, I was too weak to do this on my own. I had just remained in my wheelchair. Finally standing up using my sticks was such a turning point. I'm not sure anyone can ever quite understand what this meant to me.

During this difficult journey, I had two things to contend with; the emotional struggle surrounding my unwillingness to eat, but also still, the cerebral palsy. My legs had become so weak and stiff from not walking. The stiffness had always been the main issue, and in order to keep my legs as supple and mobile as possible I had to exercise them often.

The relief and elation I felt, being able to stand again, having spent over a month not being able to walk, was enormous. The nurses only allowed me to do a little bit of exercise once a day unfortunately and they monitored it. I think it's quite common for people with an eating disorder to obsessively exercise to try and keep their weight down, and the nurses weren't going to allow this to happen. A couple of times they caught me doing more than I should, but it was worth it, just to experience walking again.

When I wasn't eating or being observed I spent time alone in my room. One day, I sat there, staring out of the window thinking how much I wanted people to realise what a struggle it had been. I found it hard to talk about it so I wrote all my feelings down on a piece of paper. The words just came tumbling out onto the paper from my mind, and they began to rhyme, just like a poem. It was brilliant. I had never been very good at getting my point across when I spoke, so committing words to paper, to write, was perfect for me. It was such a relief to let out all my thoughts and frustrations in this way.

I called my parents and read my first poem to them. They

told me how good it was and how proud they were, which meant the world to me. My sisters also loved my poetry and told me this with their own pride in their voices. I never knew I could even write poetry, but it took this difficult journey, this struggle in my life, to find poetry within me. Who would think that such a positive outcome would appear after such a low time? I would never have thought to write poetry before the illness. It gave me a feeling of complete achievement, which just buzzed through my veins.

Finally, after nearly two months of being in the unit, the doctors discharged me and told me that I could go home. I was on the road to recovery, but life was still hard, and it took me a long time to adjust to living independently again in the big outside world. However, I got there, with support from my family and from my newfound love for poetry and self-expression.

I was determined to carry on writing poetry; I didn't want the poetry to just be about how I had struggled. I kept this promise to myself, and I am still writing poetry ten years on. I write about literally anything. I have entered competitions and have had some of my poems published. It was a very proud moment to see my poetry in a published and printed book. From then on, the poems kept flowing and my face was glowing.

Below is a poem I wrote about what I went through, about what a struggle it was being ill. I want people to know that no matter how low you are and how long you think recovery will take, there will always be light at the end of the tunnel. However, it is a journey.

Journey

I feel myself going down a slope
Then realized I couldn't cope, but lived in hope
As time went by the sky was high
I wished I could fly

As I look out the window, I can see birds mingle
The clouds are dark and white and they're moving at a great height
I can see a smile, I want to run a mile
I reach for my sticks but get in a big fix
I walk very slow, it only happens for a mo.
As I begin to go with the flow.

I'm getting stronger and feel free
And begin to feel me again.
I need to chill and not go downhill
And keep in sight the big fight.

I walk, walk, walk, with pride
Which I cannot hide
I stumble with a smile
But save myself from getting stuck in a pile.

I carry on getting there
But life hasn't been fair
I need to move on
Which I plan to do
It may be slow
This I know
And think ho ho ho ho
Suz is coming back
But needs her brain intact
Which is a fact.

A big smile on my face
Makes me want to win this AWESOME race
And this is what I will do
Which I know is OK for all of you.

Chapter 9

Losing a special part of me

In October 2014 Pips became ill with what she thought was probably flu or some sort of nasty virus. She had a temperature and had to stay in bed for most of the October half-term. I remember specifically that it was during the October half-term because we had been thinking of going away for a couple of nights with my other sister, Rosie, and her family, but Pips later said that she never would have been able to go away; she felt too ill and was confined to bed. I realised that she must have felt awful because even when Pips had been ill in the past, she was usually still up and about. It took a lot to take her down. However, this time, she told me that all she wanted to do was sleep.

We kept in contact regularly by text, email or the phone. I remember on one phone call and Pips said, 'Suz, my side is really hurting!'

I could hear the pain in her voice.

'Pips, if it gets any worse, please, please go to the doctors,' I replied.

'I will, Suz.'

I was concerned, but I didn't want Pips to pick up on this. We chatted a little more, and then said goodbye. The weeks passed, and Pips wasn't getting any better. She went to the doctors, and they said that she had a viral infection.

My sister Rosie told me that she bumped into Pips at the local leisure centre one weekend in December. Rose had been concerned about Pips too, especially as they used to meet up on a regular basis so their children could play together, cousins all meeting up and having fun! Rose told me that she hadn't seen Pips for a while, because Pips didn't feel well enough to meet up. When Rose saw Pips at the leisure centre this weekend, she said that Pips really didn't look well. She said it was hard to describe what 'not looking well' looked like, but she said that Pips just had an aura about her; it was as if Pips was troubled.

Pips told Rose about how frustrated she was with not feeling well and with having not felt right for a few months, since the October half-term. Rose said that Pips genuinely looked confused and on reflection, scared. She told Rose that she had completely lost her appetite but couldn't understand why she was so bloated. She had pointed out her abdomen. Rose later told me that although she didn't say anything to Pips, she did notice that Pips did look bloated. Rose said that she just looked gaunt.

It was on Christmas Eve that Barry, her husband called us all to tell us that Pips was in hospital following heart failure. She had collapsed at Salisbury Playhouse just before heading in to watch a pantomime. Pips had mentioned to me earlier in the week that she couldn't wait to take Evangeline to watch the pantomime, but she also said she still wasn't feeling well. However, she was determined to see the pantomime. I was sitting at my desk, just about to turn off my computer when I got the call. It was quite late in the evening so I did wonder who it could be, calling so late.

'Pips is in hospital,' were Barry's words to me.

My heart sank.

'Oh no, what's wrong with her, Barry?' I asked.

He explained that she had collapsed just before going in to

watch the pantomime and that the tests she had upon arriving at the hospital revealed that she had experienced heart failure. I started crying. I couldn't believe what I was hearing. Barry was comforting and said that he didn't think it was anything too serious, just the aftermath of this virus that she had.

However, the question that still loomed for us all was, 'Why, why had her heart failed?'

Christmas Day was very strange without Pips. We all knew that she would want the children to have fun, so we tried to enjoy ourselves and make it fun for them, especially Evangeline, who must have been so worried about her mummy.

Pips was on my mind constantly. I just wanted to be with her. The room felt empty, despite all the chatter. We took a family photo, but it was incomplete without Pips. I hate having my photo taken, so I did try to get out of it, but no such luck! I wish I could just run on these occasions! Before we all went home to our respective houses after a busy but worried Christmas Day, we had a silent moment and thought of Pips.

The next day, Barry kindly took me to see Pips in the hospital. I couldn't wait. I knew I had to try to keep it together for her, though. We did have a laugh, but I could tell she was in pain. I noticed all the wires that connected her to numerous monitors, and there was a drip in her arm. Despite all this discomfort and all the uncertainty surrounding why she was even in hospital, she still insisted on asking how I was. She didn't want to talk about herself.

We did share quite a giggle when I returned from the loo, because I told her how the light in the loo was on a timer, and if you didn't move for a while, the light went off. I was telling her about this, explaining how I had to sit in the loo in the dark, because I didn't know what to do! I didn't realise that I needed to activate the sensor again, so I just sat there and wondered how long I would be stuck here for! I wasn't anywhere near the basin and because I can't stand unaided, I didn't want to risk moving in the dark, when I couldn't see anything. So, I had to just stay where I was and hope that the light would come back on! Thankfully it did! It must have eventually detected some movement from me! Pips and I did laugh quite a bit about this. Visiting time was over too quickly, and I had to say goodbye to Pips, promising I would come back as soon as I could to see her. She said she would keep in touch over text messaging. On the journey home, I was quiet and very upset.

After a few days, Pips came home as she was making a good recovery following the heart failure. The heart failure was initially put down to a virus – the virus that her body had been fighting for all these months, making her feel so unwell. However, when Pips went for an MRI scan to check the recovery of her heart, the results from this revealed a recovered heart, but also a large mass under her arm. Pips was aware of this mass but wasn't hugely concerned because she had thought it was just a gland linked to this awful virus.

The tests began; the doctors took a biopsy, and all we could do was wait.

Once Pips had settled back home and spent some time resting and being with Barry and Evangeline, I called her and asked if I could pop over.

'Of course you can!' she told me.

She seemed pleased to have visitors. It was still a complete waiting game – waiting for the test result to come back from the biopsy that had been done on this large mass under her arm.

'The house is being cleaned though; do you mind?' she asked tentatively.

'Of course not,' I said. 'See you shortly!'

I called for a taxi, which thankfully didn't take long to arrive. They secured me and my wheelchair in the back and off we drove to Pips' house. I could barely wait the thirty minutes that it took to get there and out of the taxi at Pips' house. When I arrived, Barry helped me into their house. It's a good job he is strong as he near enough lifted me and my chair up the few steps to their front door!

Pips greeted me with a kiss as she always did. I also met her cleaners. Barry soon got the coffee on, and Pips and I sat and chatted. We had a photo taken together and this time I didn't jump as I usually did when the flash of the camera goes off! And I managed to keep my eyes open; another automatic reaction that I get when I hear the click of the camera or the flash of the light – my eyes instantly shut!

We chatted for a while. Pips always took such an interest in what I had been doing. I didn't stay for that long because Pips was tired, and I knew how important it was for her to rest. As I was leaving Pips said, 'When will I see you again, Suz?'

'Soon, very soon,' I promised.

'I hope it won't be too late,' she replied.

This made me well up inside. Pips still didn't look well at all, and I think we were all incredibly concerned that the doctors had thought it was necessary to do a biopsy on this lump under her arm. We knew they were testing for cancer. We just all wanted her to get better.

The taxi came and took me home. I texted Pips when I got back, as I always did, to let her know I was home and to thank her for having me over. We both finished the text with 'I love you'.

I then sat in silence and cried. I cried for ages. I kept going over the conversation we had earlier, about when we were next going to see each other and Pips saying that she hoped it wouldn't be too late. Why did she say that, I asked myself. I just had a feeling that Pips knew something was seriously wrong with her. Later that evening I called my parents to say that I had been to see Pips. They were visiting Pips every day, so even though I couldn't see Pips every day, I was getting regular updates on how she was doing from both my parents and my other two sisters, who were also keeping in touch with Pips daily.

On Wednesday, January 7th, exactly two weeks after the

heart failure episode on Christmas Eve, Pips was told that the biopsy had confirmed a malignant tumour under her arm that they couldn't operate on. Even more devastating was that this wasn't the primary cancer. This was secondary cancer, which had spread. The doctors told Pippa that the primary cancer was likely to be breast cancer, but Pips had never felt a lump in her breast.

I cried every night. I can't imagine or put into words how Pips and the family must have felt. I just couldn't get my head around it. Pips stayed fit and healthy; she was always out running or riding her bike, and what about Evangeline, their lovely daughter. Pips and Evangeline were so close, inseparable.

Treatment began straight away, and we all remained very positive, particularly as the doctors told Pips that the tumour under her arm was shrinking each week. She had decided to use a 'cold cap' whilst she was administered the chemotherapy. This was to try to prevent hair loss. Pips had to wear this cap, chilled to between minus 15 and minus 40-degree Fahrenheit for a little while before the treatment, during the treatment, and for a little while after. She sent us all a picture of her wearing the cold cap.

Pips was always very exhausted after the treatment and would go straight home and rest. As the days progressed, her energy levels would pick up and she was able to get jobs done, go shopping, take a walk or visit people. She had regular blood tests to confirm how her body was responding to the treatment. It was looking positive; the levels of cancerous cells had reduced significantly, and the lump was shrinking by the week.

Ironically, a month or so after the treatment had started, I found a lump under my arm. When I went to get it checked, the GP suggested that I have a mammogram. I didn't tell Pips for a while; she was going through enough and I didn't want to worry her. I had spoken to Jenny and Rose about it, and my mother.

My appointment was quick to come through. One day, when I was visiting Pips, I decided to tell her about the appointment.

'I want to come with you, Suz,' she told me.

'Are you sure, Pips?' I replied. 'You've got enough going on.'

'I'm sure, Suz,' she said.

I was so grateful to Pips. I knew she wasn't at all well, but she insisted on coming with me. I was quite sure that she wouldn't have offered if she didn't feel she could face it.

When the day arrived, Pips was true to her word and met me at the hospital. As we sat waiting for the doctor, Pips said to me, 'Suz, I really hope you don't have this; that you don't have what I've got.'

Neither of us could bear to say the word cancer.

'It's awful and I'm worried about how you would cope,'

I think between us, we were both wondering whether the twin connection was in play again, and that we were going to experience something so awful at the same time, just as we had experienced so many other aspects of life together. Maybe a part of me wanted to go through this at the same time with her, so I could be there for Pips and fully understand how she was feeling.

The results from the mammogram confirmed that the lump under my arm was nothing to be concerned about, but I was reassured that it was sensible of me to have had it checked. Pips looked at me and said, 'Thank goodness, Suz. Thank goodness. I just don't think you could have coped.'

I just looked at Pips and we hugged one another. I felt so sad for Pips. It was all just so unfair. After my appointment, we went along to the ward that Pips had to visit regularly for an injection. She introduced me to all the nurses; they all seemed very nice, but to be honest, I felt as if I was living through a nightmare; I just couldn't believe that Pips had cancer. I tried to remain strong around Pips, but I think she knew that I had been crying.

'What's wrong, Suz?' she would ask.

'Nothing, Pip, I'm ok. Don't worry about me,' I would reply.

We were all just praying that this chemotherapy would cure her – would take this cancer away from her, would make her well again. I didn't realise that there were so many different types of chemotherapy, depending on the type of cancer, and I didn't realise how important it was to get the treatment right for each patient. Pips just wanted to get on with things and tried to do the best that she could, but she was feeling so ill. She very much wanted to be with her family and to have everyone near to her, to keep in contact with us all. My other two sisters would pop by and see Pips after work. I felt useless in all honesty because I couldn't find a reliable taxi that would take me to see Pips, and then it was hard for me to manage around their house due to my wheelchair. My legs don't cope with stairs well, and there were a few of them just to get to Pips' front door. I knew Pips understood though. I still called or texted her every day.

Despite the treatment seemingly working on the tumour, the cancer was still spreading. Following another MRI scan, the doctors told Pips that there were signs of it in her bones, particularly at the bottom of her spine. They advised her that she would need to take special medication for the rest of her life to control the spread of cancer in the bones.

Pips then began to lose her ability to speak. Her words began to slur, and she couldn't understand why this was. It was so frustrating for her. There was a thought that it might be the impact of the chemotherapy, so the doctors suggested that she take a break from the treatment. She was terrified that taking a break from the treatment would cause the tumour to grow again. However, she took the advice. She was feeling so unwell by this point.

There was one day that I knew Pips was not right, that she was in a bad place. I texted her in the morning to tell her that I was thinking of her.

'Thinking of you. Lots of love and hugs' was what I wrote.

By the afternoon I still hadn't heard back from Pips; she hadn't replied to my text, which was unusual. My mind went into overload. I decided to text my eldest sister, Jen, to ask if she knew how Pips was. I knew that Jen had been seeing Pips regularly. Jen texted back and as I read the words 'Pips can't speak very well; her speech is slurred, and she's finding it difficult to hold anything', I realised that Pips was very ill.

Now that Pips couldn't text me, I had to rely on my sisters to keep me updated, which they did, but it did mean that there were gaps in what I knew between the time of receiving that text message from Jen and next seeing Pips. Being in a wheelchair was so restrictive, and it was hard to book taxis, which meant that because I couldn't see Pips and she wasn't able to keep in touch over the phone or through text, I was less aware of Pips' rapid and cruel decline. Pips literally went from chatting and having guests over to not being able to walk up her own stairs in a matter of days.

On Saturday, May 2nd, the doctors admitted Pips to the oncology ward at Salisbury hospital. She was very ill and unable to speak, and she was drifting in and out of consciousness. Just two days earlier she had been sitting on the sofa, albeit weak, but able to communicate and interact. The doctors gave Pips some steroids, which helped her regain consciousness. By Thursday, May 7th the doctors confirmed that Pips' illness was terminal. My father phoned me to let me know that the doctors only gave Pips a few weeks more to live.

Pips went into the hospice on May 9th, a Saturday afternoon. My father came to pick me up so that we were all together with Pips. He had arranged for me to use one of the hospice's wheelchairs, which was a real help. Pips was in a room on her own, which had a lovely view from the window. If Pips could have seen that view, she would have loved it.

When my father pushed me into the room I said, 'Hi, Pips. It's Suz.'

She opened her eyes and gave me a small smile then closed her eyes. She knew that we were all by her side, and that's where we all stayed. The hospice staff were so kind to Pips and all of us. They suggested we took it in turns to sit with Pips and offered us other places in the hospice to rest. We didn't know how long we would be there, but none of us wanted to leave.

They explained to us what to look out for as Pips moved towards the end of her life; what her final breaths might be like, what they might sound like. I couldn't keep it together, but I had to try for Pips, like the rest of the family were doing.

Pips was never alone. We all took it in turns to be by her side. I was holding her hand and kissing it. I'm sure she knew it was me. I didn't want to leave. The hospice allowed families to bring their pets in, so Truccles, Pips' dog, that she adored, was able to stay with her too.

At one point, it was just Rosie and me sitting with Pips, holding her hand whilst talking to her. Rosie started playing some music from her phone. She played the theme tune to *Gladiator*, 'Now We Are Free'. It was such a lovely idea and heartbreakingly apt. Rosie was talking in a very soft voice to Pips; telling Pips quietly that she could let go. Rosie was reminding Pips of how when she gave birth, she was told to relax and just let go then, and that now, she had to do the same. She had to relax and let her body take over. She was telling Pippa that everything was going to be ok. I noticed Pips' breathing becoming more relaxed. We continued to listen to music. Pips loved music, just like I do. We liked similar music.

Later that afternoon a vicar came to give a blessing to Pips. We were around her bed, holding her hands and each other's. It was incredibly emotional but beautifully done. I still couldn't believe Pips was going to die. After the blessing, I stayed with Pips whilst people were making hot drinks. I sat and held her hand and kissed it, and I was talking about the things we used to do together. When we were in our early twenties, we used to regularly meet up and go to Tesco's cafe for a cuppa and a doughnut. I reminded her of this. We had always enjoyed these times together.

The family had returned with the teas and coffees. The soft

chatting continued. The hospice staff often popped their heads in to see if we were all ok. Every hour or so, they would move Pips into a different position, so she wouldn't get bed sores. We all left the room at this point but returned as soon as they had finished. I could hear them talking gently to Pips. I'm sure she could hear what they were saying. On one occasion when they turned her, the nurses had put a different nightie on Pips and combed her hair. I think she would have liked the nightie and might have even chosen it herself. I thought, 'Great minds think alike.'

Pips kept coughing; I'm not sure why. The doctor gave her some medicine to make it more comfortable for her. The doctor talked us through everything, like what to expect as Pips took her final breaths. Every single member of staff at the hospice was so kind and supportive. Tragically, we all knew that it was just a matter of time now. Pips was being so strong; it was like she didn't want to give up. She didn't appear to be in pain; the only noticeable struggle was her breathing, which was becoming slower and slower. Barry stayed with Pips and lay by her side, holding her hand constantly. My sisters and I made use of the guest room that had become available.

Having spent most of the night by Pips' bedside on the Saturday night, with little rest on both the Saturday and Sunday, we decided that on the Sunday evening we would all try to get some sleep. There were more guest rooms available at the hospice now, so we were able to lie down on a bed rather than doze on a chair. It was hard to leave Pips, but we agreed that should there be any change in her condition, the nurse would come and wake us up immediately.

I didn't want to leave Pips. I wanted to be with her all the time. Eventually, I convinced myself to leave Pips' bedside and try to get some sleep. As I wheeled myself into the room, I realised that one of my worries was that if I got out of the wheelchair and lay on the bed, my legs would become so stiff that I wouldn't be able to get back up and into the wheelchair should I need to do this quickly, if Pips was nearing the end. My legs do this all the time, but at home, I have the facilities to get out of bed quicker and the time to let my legs loosen up. I didn't have this in the hospice; especially not if we were called to Pips' bedside quickly. However, I was sharing a room at the hospice with my sister Jenny, and she helped me get in and out of my wheelchair and pushed me through the hospice corridors.

The knock came just before 5am. It was Monday, May 11th, 2015. The nurse told us that Pips didn't have long left and that if we wanted to be with her, we should go to her now. Pips was ready, she had surrendered, and we just got there in time to be with her whilst she took her final breath. She died peacefully, gracefully, and we were all with her.

We then all had our own time to say goodbye to Pips. To sit with her, alone, but this time she wasn't breathing. I was just numb. I couldn't believe it; I just couldn't believe it. Again, the hospice staff were so fantastic, totally understanding of our need to be by Pips' side to say our final goodbyes and to offer us their support, which was often an arm around our shoulder, or soothing words, whilst we cried. Everything that the hospice offered us is exactly as Pips would have wanted and was everything that we needed.

There was a church service a few weeks later to celebrate Pips' life. Over three hundred people attended; Pips would have been so proud. It was a warm, sunny day. Rose read a poem that she had made especially for Pips, and Jen read a passage from the Bible. Barry did an emotional eulogy, and beautiful Evangeline read *Guess How Much I Love You* by Sam McBratney. We sang some wonderful hymns, one being 'I Danced in the Morning', which Pips and Barry had at their wedding, and another being 'Thy Hand Oh God Has Guided' which has become a family hymn. We also listened to some of Pips' favourite songs. The most memorable for me are the ones by Ed Sheeran, 'All the Stars' and 'Thinking Out loud'. After the service, we all mingled in the churchyard, in the sunshine, chatting and sharing our memories of Pips.

We had another service for Pips the next day at the Salisbury crematorium. This was just for the family. It was incredibly emotional. Again, we sang some lovely hymns, including 'Lead us Heavenly Father Lead Us'. During the final song, 'Run' by Leona Lewis, my parents helped me walk to the coffin. I put my hand on it, gave a kiss, and said my final goodbye.

My parents waited just over a week to receive Pips' ashes and arranged for an interment of them at St Peter's Church, in Winterbourne Stoke. This was where my grandparents had lived, and where my aunt still lives, in the farmhouse that we had spent so many memorable weekends and half-terms, whilst my parents were in Zimbabwe or living far away from our schools. We visit there on our birthday and on the anniversary of Pips' death. My parents organised a beautiful gravestone, which has the following words on the flat stone:

'No pain no grief nor anxious fears can reach our loved ones sleeping here.'

The intention for this resting place for Pips is that it is a family gravestone, and so it provides a place for others in the family to join Pips when their time comes, if they so wish. Pips would like to know that in her new creation she would not be alone.

I find life so hard now without Pips. I feel empty and so very sad. Writing poetry has kept me going, so when I'm feeling low, I take myself away from it all and just concentrate on writing. Sometimes the words just flow, and I feel a form of release. I wrote a poem in memory of Pips, shortly after Pips had passed away. It's called 'A Shining Star'. Writing this poem meant so much, and it gave me a way to express how I feel and to write about Pips, who she was and what she meant to me. I have a copy of this poem in my flat, on the wall. It has a lovely photo of Pips in the background behind the words, with a scattering of 'forget-menots' in the background too. Pips also loved my poetry. When my love for poetry first began, after I became ill, Pips always showed such an interest in reading the poems that I had written.

There are no words in the dictionary that can describe how I feel after losing a special part of me, after losing my twin. I now call the birthday that we share, 'Pips Day'. We all go to the family grave and spend time with her on our birthday, and we go there to remember the day that she passed away, on May 11th. We also visit on Pips' and Barry's wedding anniversary. I want to feel as if I am near her, and I feel this when I am at this special place.

I dream about Pips often. It is so nice to dream about her; it makes me feel as if we're together again. We have lots of fun in our dreams. We are usually running together, and even though in the dream I am able-bodied, she always wins! Another recurring dream I have is of Pips and I being with friends in a pub and I order another Smirnoff Ice! Pips then says, 'Are you getting a bit drunk, Suz?!'

I think both dreams represent the good times we had together and the life I wish I'd had with her as an able-bodied person. When I wake up from these dreams, I want to text her but quickly realise I can't.

I often wonder where you go after you die. I want to know where Pips is, but it all comes down to a belief or a faith in some sort of afterlife. We'll never really know. Rose has a Christian faith and believes that Pips is now in heaven, at peace with her maker, free of pain and the complexities of life. I know that Barry has a similar faith in God, as did Pips. Pips was very much part of her own local church, and Rosie's church community also knew her, Barry and Evangeline well. Pips was always open about her faith and often told me that she prayed a lot. She had been part of an Alpha course, a forum where people can explore their faith to a deeper level, ask questions and just engage in lengthy discussions about religion. Barry also joined her in this.

My time at Treloars didn't hugely install the Christian faith in me as I was growing up, not in the same way that it was inaugurated within my sister's upbringing; they all went to a catholic school with nuns. So, following Pips' passing away, I have really questioned my beliefs and have searched in my heart for where I really think Pips is. I often look up to the sky to talk to Pips, day or night. If it's during the day, I see the sun as being Pips, and Pips is smiling. When it rains, I think that Pips is sleeping! But mostly, I see the sun, and I see Pips. At night she's the stars, and she's the brightest one up there. But my true comfort is upon sight of a robin. Pips is in every robin I see. I suppose I believe in an element of reincarnation, because I often wonder if Pips' soul is in the robin; maybe Pips has come back as a robin, so she can fly freely and be wherever she wants to be. When I see a robin, I'm sure it stays still for that extra moment longer, hoping to connect with me. I feel this is reflective of the connection that Pips, and I shared not only whilst in the womb, but throughout our life together. We had a wave of twin telepathy when we lived our life on earth together, and the connection I feel with a robin when I see one brings back that same feeling of an unspoken connection, and a feeling of telepathy. I often say, 'Hello' to the robin, sometimes 'Hello, Pips', and on more than one occasion, when I say this, the robin turns its head to look at me.

I love you Pips and miss you so much. I wrote this for you.

A Shining Star

As I look to the sky, the clouds are high
I just want to say "hi" not "goodbye"
You will always be in our hearts Pips, that's why
Keeping an eye just like a butterfly.

Pips you were a part of me and always will be
I will never forget the things you did for me
Pips had a heart of gold that everyone could see

Caring for people was your priority and happened naturally.

Pips you always kept fit and wore a colourful cycling kit
So everyone could see you racing along happily
You often cycled over to me then texted to say you were here safely
Then a flavoured tea was on the agenda for me and we chatted happily
We were as relaxed as can be, it was lovely juvly.

Pips you were always on the go, but would never forget people tho.
And would make time to see people when you had a mo.
Or ring them to let them know you couldn't show
We all miss chatting to you, you'll always be in the "Dru Drury crew"
It's not the same without you.

Our driving tests were on the same day
Twin telepathy was working well, I have to say
Amazing hey, in my area the sky was grey
It wasn't my day but green lights came "Pips way"
A white Fiat Panda went cruising every day
No tickets were issued along the way, brilliant hey
Let's go to Tesco's we would both say
We took turns to pay and laughed lots on the way.

I remember doing a charity swim and the local paper popped in
Oh I had a grin from chin to chin and did a length in a min.
Without you they wouldn't have come in, your support helped me win.

I miss you every day, more than words can say
A big part of my heart has been torn away
We will be re-united one day.

"Keep going, Suz" I hear you say
Enjoy your flavoured drinks today
But keep the exercising at bay.
Pips you're a shining star and that will always stay
When I visit you, I hear the birds singing away.

Chapter 10

The future

None of us can ever know what the future holds. We can reflect on the past, move on from the past and enjoy concentrating on the moment of 'now' and keeping positive about the future. We don't know what other events are going to take place in our tapestry of life, but we must try to embrace it all and keep smiling.

My past has been an interesting one, and it has been unusual; not just because of having cerebral palsy, but also being a twin, and then having such a close age gap between Pips and me, and Jenny. Then Rosie adding to our family all those years later. The experience of boarding school was also a unique experience, and it is now in my adult years that I can reflect and appreciate how much it offered me in terms of independence and preparing me for the outside world.

I look back on my life and can see that despite the battles and the grief that I encountered, it's been a life of achievements and happiness. A life where I have far exceeded what other people said I could ever accomplish, starting from being able to sit up and walk, when even that was in question when I was a baby. I met the three goals my parents and I set out when I left school, and although I no longer drive or work, I still live independently. I manage my own shopping, I cook for myself, I organise my days out, I book a taxi if I need to go out, or I catch a bus. I proved to those people that said I couldn't do it, that I could. I proved that I could keep up and, in many cases, surpass that of an able-bodied person; for example, swimming a marathon. I spent many years out of the water, due to a lack of confidence and body image issues, however, I have recently started swimming again. I now swim most days, and usually do over thirty lengths. I just love swimming; I feel so free and it is a great way of keeping fit whilst also being gentle on my muscles.

Before I took to the water again, I completed a walking challenge to raise some money for the hospice that so kindly looked after Pips. I completed it during the global pandemic in 2020 when there wasn't much option to do any other sport. I walked seven hundred laps of the corridor outside my flat, each lap required me to walk about fifteen steps. I was so proud and pleased that I could give something back to the community of people who made Pips' last days ones of comfort, peace and dignity.

I wrote a poem about this challenge:

A Challenge I Will Never Forget

Exercise is what I enjoy to do
It helps my cerebral palsy too
Which is good in my view
And the circulation flows through
So my legs don't turn blue.

I've had an idea that I'll pursue
It's something I am really into
Buying shoes is an expensive issue
Now, there is a BIG clue.

A walking challenge is new
Seven hundred laps is just a few
There is no giving up it's true
Pips it's for you and Salisbury Hospice too
I'll email the fundraising area that's who
Which I will do after a brew.

I get a reply within a minute or two
The team are such a lovely crew
They offer to send me a T-shirt too
Then I set up a Just Giving page how cool
Checking the information is the first rule
Social media is a good advertising tool
Posters were made so everyone knew
It's on the 20th September, so training I mustn't overdo
Leading up to "A CHALLENGE I WILL NEVER FORGET"
just flew
And the donations kept flowing though. I'm humbled it's true.

On the day I start with a sway no one gets in my way
I hope my walking will get better throughout the day
And the stiffness in my legs will go, I pray
Then I can "jog in Suz style" hey
While the video is on play, it's great I say.

I've found my rhythm I hope it will stay
I'm reaching my target which is okay
Six hundred and eighty before midday
Gosh, I can't believe it is over halfway
I'll upload some pictures anyway
I will do this without delay.

I have twenty laps left to do
Before I know it, I'm on the final two

This is a "CHALLENGE I WILL NEVER FORGET" it's true.

As I walk to my chair I wish Pips was there
My emotions are everywhere
I have got a picture of her to share
She liked to exercise in the fresh air
And ran for charities when she had time to spare.

Now I have finished I write a note so everyone is aware
I receive messages of support and care
I've put the money in a safe place this was easy to prepare
If I lost the money I'd be in despair
And for all it would be unfair.

Next I meet Tamsin and Dave a great working pair
We chat outside whilst a presentation takes place there
I stand by my chair praying the wind doesn't blow my hair
If I fall what a nightmare so I say "Please Don't" in a prayer
"Oh my days" I'm still standing which is rare.

The picture is on my wall I see it and stare
And the money I raised will be helpful somewhere
I've achieved a VERY personal goal yeah
I'm glad my legs didn't give in. I told them don't you dare
I will ALWAYS remember this day to be fair
Thank you to ALL your support and care.

What I often reflect on is that I achieved everything that I set out to do, and I maintained the three goals my parents and I had agreed, for a significant period of my life. Employment and driving didn't continue, but I'm so thankful that I did have the chance to work, drive and live independently in my earlier years; otherwise, I never would have known that I could have achieved these in the same way that any other able-bodied person can.

Selection of Poems

In this final part of my book, I have included a number of poems that I have written, relating to many different experiences, thoughts and feelings that I have had over the years. The poems range from watching brilliant performances at some of my local art and city centres, to visiting special places, to wearing different clothes, to eating various foods, and to being with family and visiting certain places.

They are unique to Suz DD and writing them has kept me going during times that were tough.

I start with a poem about writing poetry and what it means to me.

I hope you enjoy them.

Poetic Suz

I love writing poetry
It chills me out no end
And doesn't send me around the bend.

I tend to let my feelings out
'cos to me, that's what poetry is all about
When I go with the flow, that's when I write best you know
I go to my PC, my mind runs free, there is a "buzzing" feeling inside of me.

I try to rhyme line by line, at times this works fine
The "Cool Dude" you see has a hidden quality
In a booklet especially designed for me
Or in a word package updated regularly
"I'm on the money", my quotes sometimes are funny.

When I'm in "The Zone", I switch off all my phones
And wonder why I can't hear any tones
It makes me crack on, otherwise the Poetic Suz will be gone
But, hopefully not for long, then I can hear a song
And it says "Let's bring it on"

I hit the send button for friends and family to see
A completed poem done by me
You'll have a pressie in your inbox
Just wait and see, it will be from Suz DD
Oh how "AWESOME" this document will be
So please treasure it, I only have one copy you see.

I have a lush feeling, it's so healing
That the poems I write are appealing
It gives my heart a kick start

And I jump to the ceiling
Oh, this is "off the hooks" true meaning.

I wrote this next poem about lava lamps. I love lava lamps and have spent some time watching them as they change colour. I find them so relaxing.

Bright Lights

When the evening is here
My lava lamp appears
Polished and cleaned thanks to "Mr Sheen"
I turn it on and wait patiently
Oh something is happening, this is good to see
The yellow and purple wax blend superbly.

Circles and bubbles form
When the wax warms
"Bright Lights" is what I see
This is pretty and relaxing for me
"The Lava Lamp" was invented in 1963
It definitely gets the thumbs up from me
And makes my flat feel cosy.

This poem is about watching a tribute Fleetwood Mac band at our local City Hall. It was definitely a night to remember!

A Night to Remember

Watch out, watch out
"The Crazy Two" are out tonight
The City Hall will be packed
"Fleetwood Mac" will make sure of that
We all take our seats and wake our feet
Ready to tap to the "WICKED" beat
My legs have had a bonus work out this week.

The introductions begin
We wonder what songs they will sing
We will keep guessing
"Everywhere" is one
I haven't heard this song for so long.

The songs continue to flow
My arms want to dance
So off they go
But where is my rhythm? I just don't know
But hey I am loving this show
The lighting makes the room glow.

I love the solo singing
And the instruments too
The "Fleetwood Mac" talent
Shines through, they interact
with their audience and make
You feel welcome too
It was a "Top night" I was
Smiling all the way through.

I had to write about Christmas time. I love seeing the children so happy and excited. It's a magical time for them.

Christmas Time

Christmas time is here
Everything is glittery at this time of year
The lights on the tree I love to see
And children are always so happy
They look forward to putting their stockings out
There is excitement about Santa coming tonight
So children without a good night's sleep, will always keep us on our feet.

The unwrapping of presents is all around
Smiles are everywhere, it is grand
Santa has been a busy bee
And is tired and ready for a camomile tea
But hopes all the children are happy
And is getting ready for next year you see.

I went through a stage of wearing beanies. These are soft hats which 'hug' the head. I had many of them and the brighter the better!

It's a Colourful Life

Life has its ups and downs
Challenges are all around
Solutions can always be found
Bright colours are always on my mind
My Beanies are cool and bright too
I wear them every day, people stop me and say
"Your hats brighten up my day". "Thank you" I say
People can see me from far away
Which is a good thing with the traffic today
Yellow and blue are my favourites too
I like a colourful life
It makes me feel positive in everything that I do
The saying "Life is what you make it" is so true.

I went with my sister, Rose and her husband to see a comedian called Laurence Clark at our local Arts Centre. Laurence also has cerebral palsy and went to Lord Mayor Treloar College. It was a great evening. He is so funny.

Comedy Night

Off to Salisbury Arts Centre I go
"A Comedian" is there that I know
So laughter will be in full flow
I am really looking forward to the show
So taxi let's go!

I arrive in plenty of time
I talk to some school friends of mine
A coffee is the next plan
Rose has it all in hand.

There is a screen on the wall
So the pictures can been seen by all
With just a click, the pictures flick
PowerPoint has its uses after all.

We all take our seats I feel upbeat
And talk away about my school days
The lights go dim, what's happening
We clap the "Host in"
And the "Health Hazard" show begins.

Confidence should be the key
When it comes to the NHS you see
Operations are performed but not before a diagram is drawn
Is this to help them with their art, or so they get the right part?

Off to America you go with your show

The camera is ready to roll
"Free Healthcare" is your goal
But the Americans said "oh no"
That didn't stop you
You're a fighter you know
It was an "Off The Hook Show"

Although this poem is titled 'Dreams', it is also about a time that I went to Paris with my boyfriend at the time. I often dreamt that I went back there.

Dreams

As I get comfy to go to sleep
My body adapts to the evening heat
I lay on my hands but always cover my feet
I always listen to my heart beat before I drift off to sleep.

What will I dream about tonight
Will it be about past events?
This at times makes me feel tense
Like the feeling I'm about to fall off a fence
This doesn't fill me with much confidence.

As I awake to a bright sunny day
And the beautiful sound of the birds singing away
My dream slowly comes back to me
Paris was where I went it was lovely juvly.

The "Eurostar" was an experience for me
I have never seen doors shut so quickly
Running is not easy for me
But I did enjoy the ride eventually.

There were lots of places to see
"The Eiffel Tower" was top of the list for me
I couldn't miss this opportunity
As I was in this romantic city with great company.

I love it when true dreams come back to me
Especially when they are happy

I wonder what my next dream will be
Full of lovely thoughts hopefully
I will just have to wait and see
Where my mind takes me.

This poem is about Christmas time at my sister's house (Rose). El Gastor was the name of their house and we used to all meet there every Christmas day. It was a Christmas routine. Blaze is Rose's dog, and Truccles is Barry, Pips and Evangeline's dog. We always had such fun on this day. Lots of noise, chatter and children playing.

Festive Fun

"El Gastor" was the meeting point on Christmas Day
"Suz" arrived early and had a lovely chat on the way
William and Hugo came to say hello
Then to the piano William goes and the music just flowed
"Happy Birthday" was played fantastically
You will be on "Britain's Got Talent"
This is where you deserve to be
And Simon Cowell would agree with me.

Blaze came to say hello
Smiling away what a lovely start to a festive day
I think mischief is coming my way
My wheelchair brakes have been serviced today
Blaze did them in a special way
And found them tasty I have to say
Then Truccles came to play.

Father and I talked away
We haven't forgotten your birthday present by the way
Do you want your poems framed in any special way
This is another exciting project I have to say
A few examples will be on the way
After the bank holiday.

Pips' iPad comes out, Jeff's about
Talking away about how technology improves every day

Jeff gets his new phone, demos are shown
Father is impressed by the phone
Mother and Father need one at home.

My niece and nephews play
It has been a "good in the hood day"
We all exchange presents and call it a day
Suz's taxi is on its way.

I had to write a poem about "I'm a Celebrity, Get Me Out Of Here". I loved watching it!

Jungle Life

A group of celebrities meet at a hotel
They chat away while a meal is being prepared for the day
This will keep them strong, but for how long.

Off to Australia they go
Their nerves begin to show
As the first team get on the plane
They shout we must be "insane"
To jump off this plane
After a few screams, their faces beam
This is an AWESOME team.

The second team get into their canoes
And paddle away
They will get to their destination by the end of the day
Then shout "that's our goal for today"

They all sit around the log fire
Eating beans and rice
There are lots of mice and insects too
A snake was found in the animal crew
I'm sure there will be more in the trials they do
Living outside is certainly different
To the life the Celebrities are used to.

They call it a night and zip up tight
To make sure the animals don't bite
A peaceful night was had by all
They woke to a lovely alarm call
Snakes were on the floor

Hey this is 'jungle life' after all.

A Bush Tucker Trial is set each day
Who will be the lucky one and get picked today
They vote, it's the fairest way
Everyone gets a chance
To get out of camp for the day
They meet lots of animals on the way
How many stars will we get today
I hope a good meal will be on its way
It will be a perfect end to a hard day.

The celebrity chest puts their knowledge to the test
Let's hope they get the question right
And a treat will be given tonight
If they get it wrong the treat will be gone
So their high spirits won't last for long
And the day will drag on.

Each day a celebrity finds out if they go or stay
The public vote away
And the chosen celebrity leaves camp that day
After chatting away all that's left to say is "I'm A Celebrity Get Me Out Of Here"
I have conquered some of my fears I have to say.

I also watched Big Brother a lot! So again, I had to write a poem about it.

House of Fun

Celebrity Big Brother is here
I love this time of year
The house is cool
It has a hot tub near the pool
And lots of cameras too
Big Brother is always watching you.

A secret task is set for the first housemate to carry out
General knowledge is what this task is all about
An earpiece is key to the task
Big Brother sets the questions
The housemate has to ask
In order for the task to be passed
Then they can have a few drinks at last.

Throughout their stay
Tasks are a big part of their day
It gets me watching them anyway
If they complete the task
A party maybe on the cards
The night will disappear fast.

The diary room is where they go
To let off steam or just to say hello
And to nominate people off the show
Big Brother only accepts good reasons
To why the people should go
Then they let the housemates know
So they can get ready for the eviction show.

As the group gets smaller, friendships grow
They were all strangers at the start of the show
Now the 'house of fun' is in full flow
The public have the final vote you know
To who should win the show.

I wrote earlier in this book about the stutter that I have. This poem is about the challenge I faced, having a stutter, and how it makes me feel.

A Big Challenge In My Life

When I was young my words didn't flow
I wanted them to though, it made my confidence go
I had lost my glow which made me feel low
One day it will come back though.

Often people rapped words as they passed
All I wanted to do is hide behind a mask
I knew this would be a challenging task
So I had to work at it fast, so the tears would not last.

Every time I tried to speak my heart did a triple beat
I could feel my body overheat but, I still had cold feet
Even with socks and shoes they were like the winter blues
They seem to have their own rules, silly fools.

My muscles would contract, I had no control over that
It wasn't an act. I knew my reflexes were intact
I need to relax, to bend my legs to the max
How am I going to do that? Let's sing a few of my favourite tracks.

I take a deep breath and the words begin to flow
I sing a tune as I go, this is great you know
I feel my face glow. I said stammer go, go, go
Will this work on the phone though?
Or will my nerves show?

Oh no, I hear the phone ring, I quietly sing
I will pick it up in a min, once I see who's calling in
My nerves are like the clappers so I up the sing

It is a confidence thing, will my positive mental attitude kick in?

"Hello I say" I can hear music play, it's sent my nerves away
A fluent Suz is on the way, hopefully it will stay
I may have a few sticky moments along the way
Practice makes perfect I often hear people say
It's certainly paid off for me today
My nerves are still at bay
The loneliness has gone, hooray
I knew I would get there someday
I will tackle my next challenges in a similar way.

Another reality television show that I loved to watch; The Apprentice. I had to write about this and give Lord Sugar a mention!

A Business Star

The Apprentice is back. Lord Sugar is full of good facts
Never argue back, just listen and bring the good results back
This year the show had a change of plan
The contestants could think up their own business plan
With the backing of a top business man
Lord Sugar is on hand.

The contestants are divided into two teams
They compete against one another, each have a project manager
Who delegates jobs to each members of his/her team
They let their business minds flow
With the knowledge they already know
They then say ready, steady, let's go
We're going to win this task you know.

What do the public want to see
A good invention would be useful to me
It all depends on the pitch, let's hope they deliver it without a hitch
And come back and say we sold something today.

The board room is next
Who will win, and which contestants will "The project manager bring back in"
They each give a saving speech
In the hope that they will go onto the next show
They must be so nervous waiting to know
All they want to do is to achieve their goal
And not to have to go.

The final week is here
The interviewing panel appear
And the business plans have to be clear
An inventor was hired this year
He was very sincere
And always had a notepad
To write down his ideas
He was always fair with his peers.

Another tribute band at our local City Hall. I went to quite a few, including Queen.

Bon Jovi Rock Night

Bon Jovi here we come
It's rock and roll night, what fun
We warm our chords to help our jaws
The atmosphere is first class, Bon Jovi sets us some little tasks
But oh, will my brain last I ask, in my eyes he is the singing king
So I 'Don't Want To Miss A Thing'

"Bed of Roses" comes on, oh, how I love this song
The words are great, I would love roses on a plate
And one day to find my soul mate
I hope it's not too late.

"Keep the Faith" is a grand song too, the words are so very true
I like humming it I really do, I wish "Always" was played as well
As the song has meaning to me,
To achieve is always the key
That is what people have said to me
So I try to make it my top priority.

Then "Shout" comes on, this is a very uplifting song
Bon Jovi gets us all singing and swaying along to this shouting song
His love for singing is very strong
Interacting with people is his number one
He does this fine, so as a band they will stay to shine.

This poem reflects how often I had to put my 'mind over matter', in order to stay strong and determined. It's a few words to express how I used willpower and the power of my mind to overcome my physical problems.

Mind Over Matter

My mind needs a kick
All I can hear is a small tick
I wish it could be fixed and not in this terrible mix
How can I see through this
Without seeing thick mist.

I talk away, good listeners always stay
They may offer advice, which is always nice
This I will have to see all I want is my mind to run free
And be happy, cause that's just me to a "T"
Which I know people long to see.

I have to keep strong in order to move on
Pushing my emotions aside, with no guide
This has always made me hide
Cos I don't want to lose my pride.

I used to visit Weymouth with my sisters for a few days, usually over a weekend. We would stay in the same hotel each time, which had a pool. The children loved the pool. I would sit at the side, with a cup of tea, watching them and chatting with my sisters (if they weren't in the pool!). I had stopped swimming at this time, so I didn't join them.

Weymouth Fun

Weymouth is the sea of life
With lots of spice this was very nice
Along the beach we went following the lovely sea scent.

The boys ran on the sand
And William offered to lend a hand
To push Auntie Suz, it's so grand
Kites fly high in the sky
I enjoy them whizzing by.

We see lots of shops
Via a percent I'm thinking hey chick this rocks
Brightly coloured things is what I can see
If I stay here I will feel free
But won't get back for a cup of tea.

William sits on Suz's lap
While Jeff and Rose find the way back
We seem to have lost track
We stroll along so many paths
But all the same, have lots of laughs.

We try to cross the road
In a very slow mode
Cars wait patiently to see
Where we want to be

While we all talk so freely.

William and Hugo want to play
In the pool they shout hip, hip hooray
This is where they stay
Well just for today
Mummy joins in with a spin
And says "we must get out in a min."
William shows all, that he earned top score
By swimming underwater
With our applause we don't falter.

Later it's hide and seek
This puts me right at my peak
Cos it's fun to hear laughs and counting too
William and Hugo think this is an awesome game too.

Hugo shouts "coming ready or not"
William finds a great hiding spot
Hugo searches high and low
Including head to toe.

He'll find him in a mo.
If he goes with this nice flow
They are re-united, this is fantastic to see
They have both been really busy bees
And are very good to me.

A poem just to reflect my thoughts on technology and how quickly it is moving on.

Talking TV

As I sit and watch the TV with a liquorice tea
A small square appears in the right corner, what could this be?
I wait patiently, an advert appears suddenly
There is no need to contact "The BBC"
Patience is the key, "Hello to Talking Technology"

The advert gets into full swing and pictures begin
Funny voices come in then they start to sing
Shall I call the Music King?
No they are already being counted in
I love music things so I'll be quiet for a min.
Who knows, I may learn something, then I can join in.

Wow this is interesting to me and a member of my family
Will Google find anything for me on "Talking TV's"
It's searching hard I see and finding information finally
I am as pleased as can be, now I have to read through it thoroughly
It's going to be my new hobby.

Practice, practice is the thing, then it will start happening
Deciding the product is the next thing, I'll get there in a min
I'm BUZZING, BUZZING, as ideas are coming in
It has to be eye-catching to keep the viewers tuned in, this is the main thing.

A new invention comes to mind, but what kind?
Something along the carrying lines, it's a challenge at times
A cup that clips on to my sticks, or my wheelchair bits, if I need a drinking fix

My chair will be made up ready to visit The Ritz
So to the manufacturers I go, this could go on show
I may sell lots you know, I will then have a constant glow
My autograph will be in full flow and I'll be on the go.

I ordered snacks over the internet from a company called Graze. They offered really good snacks, which I loved at the time of writing this poem.

Variety Snack Surprise

I heard an advert that interested me so I googled it on my PC
The website appeared instantly it was eye catching to me
I navigated through easily all the snacks were there to see
I'm "BUZZING" like a bee, everything is explained to a "T"
I sign up happily, what will the next stage be for "SDD"

Taking a food history is key so the right snacks are sent to me
So down the page I go, ticking things I like and know
Then there is a box flow and many different snacks show
Which one will I choose tho, I'll explore them in a mo
With just one click I can get an 'oaty' fix in the variety mix
Or a protein kick, with a seed mix and pretzel sticks.

The variety box is for me, the four snacks are placed neatly
Rating the snacks is a priority,
If I "LIKE" it will be sent regularly
"LOVE" it will be sent often, yippee,
"TRY" it will be sent occasionally, I'll wait patiently
"BIN" it's not my thing, so it won't be happening
"SEND SOON" *then another is a must, the flavours are* LUSH, LUSH.

Now it's time to set up a delivery, fortnightly suits me
I can change it if needs be, there are no ties you see
Ordering "one off boxes" is easy, there is just such flexibility
The flapjack box is one for me, it will give me lots of energy
There will be no stopping chilled DD, a flapjack box will come soon, yippee.

My variety surprise arrives, through the letterbox it slides
I try to guess the snacks inside before I see the information guides
Sometimes I get one out of four, other times none at all
One day I'll be on the ball and get four out of four.

So it's now time to see what's inside the box for me?
Banana Hazelnut and Date Bread and a tea, "LOVELY JUVLY"
As I take a bite, my taste buds excite, the flavours gel just right
It fills me with delight, I will rate this tonight
"LOVE" it will be, I will receive it often, yippee.

I have a Lemon and Poppy Slice, nice, nice, nice
It's bright and light and "BUBBLING" too, and it looks cool
I "LOVE" the flavour, I do, I can't wait to taste another it's true
Rating it as "LOVE" is what I will do.

A Banana Protein Flapjack, I can't wait to try
Bananas are a good source of energy, that's why
I like them too and they are part of the five a day rule
They have potassium in them and this is healthy for you
So I take a nibble and smile away, I'll be on top form throughout the day
The banana and mixed seeds are perfect I have to say
So rating it is easy "A MUST LUSH, LUSH SEND SOON" all the way.

"WOUZERS" Bonnie Wee Oat Bakes, I haven't heard of these before
I like cheese, chives, and red onion for sure, so I know I will adore
So guess what, it will make a "LOVE" rating once more
And it will come often through my door.

As you will know from reading "Variety Snack Surprise"

I can't believe my eyes, the snacks should get first prize
And customer services too, you all "ROCK" *you do*
There is one last word I will say to you
"ALL GOOD IN THE HOOD" *and thank you.*

This next poem is for my big sister Jenny. Jen has always been there for me. If there is a crisis, such as times when I've had to go to hospital, Jenny will always visit, but will also offer to bring me any items from home, or whilst I'm away, she'll keep my flat clean and tidy. She has a heart of gold.

Jenny and George (her husband) had a really special dog called Ruddles. In the early days, when Ruddles was a puppy, I would sometimes dog-sit him. I really enjoyed this. Here is the poem I wrote about him.

Ruddles

"Ruddles" is a Sheep Dog with a bit of Labrador too
When he was a puppy I looked after him and enjoyed it too
He loved playing with the ball
And chased it as it rolled around on the floor
Then he would stop it with his paw
And bring it back to me to roll some more
After a while he would lie on the floor
He was exhausted for sure.

"Ruddles" is a faithful dog
And would do anything for you
He loves to round up other animals
And watches every move they do
If an animal is out of line
"Ruddles" knows exactly what to do
He is patient too.

The Baylis family have other dogs too
They all look after each other, it's cool
Animals are friends for life it's true.

For my youngest sister Rose, who helped me to write this book.

Sister Love

Rose, you're a star
Your personality shines from afar
You're quick to help others
And you're very good with all the mothers
How they turn to you
When they want to talk things through
They get good advice
Which never comes at a price
It's the nature in you that makes
Things I want to say so true.

We always laugh together
This I will always treasure
You make me feel free
Oh how we just love our cups of teas
You make them just how I like them to be.

You are filled with love
Just like a million of doves
That shine from above
You're bright just like the moon at night.

I just want you to know
And for you to keep going with the flow
That I love you so and I hope this always shows.

Printed in Great Britain
by Amazon